To: Malissia

Hard Truth

The Journey of a thousand miles
begins with one step.

Lynda Ann Murray

25. June 2022.

Hard Truth

Growing out of adversity

DR. LYNDA INCE-GREENAWAY

THE CHOIR PRESS

First published in the United Kingdom in 2021 by
The Choir Press

ISBN paperback 978-1-78963-255-2

ISBN hardback 978-1-78963-256-9

ISBN ebook 978-1-78963-257-6

Contents

Dedication and Acknowledgements

A word fitly spoken is like apples of gold in pictures of silver.
PROVERBS 25:11 HOLY BIBLE, KING JAMES VERSION.

I am thankful to God for helping me to complete my book. To Him are the thanks and the Glory.

I dedicate this book to the memory of my beloved mother, Mrs. Eudora Oxley who guided and parented me. She overcame every struggle as a single parent who emigrated to England in 1963. She is congratulated and recognised posthumously for her accomplishments in raising eight children successfully after the death of her husband. She taught us how to meet and overcome life's challenges without fear and with fortitude.

I also dedicate this book to my son Dr. Michael Eaton Delisle Ince and my grandson Lenny Ince. It is because of them that my life story is worth telling.

Sadly, I dedicated this book to my brother Daryl Oxley posthumously. He showed love encouraging me to believe in my God-given abilities and was optimistic that I would publicise my story for the benefit of others. I also acknowledge the support I consistently received from my siblings, Judith Oxley, Dr. Gozil Oxley, Pauline Oxley, Denise Oxley and Joy Oxley.

I would also like to thank those who read my manuscript and gave their valuable feedback that it was a book worthy of publication.

I acknowledge the steadfast support and encouragement that my husband, Hubert Greenaway, gave me to complete my memoir.

Author's Note

This book provides insight into my life. I have provided a faithful account of my life as far as I could recall and in particular the events that had an impact on my lifelong journey. In some instances, I have changed names to protect people's identity. Real names were only used for family members or in circumstances where I was granted permission to do.

In telling my story I have adhered to accuracy; this is where it was an advantage to talk to my relatives and allow them to read the manuscript. My autobiography is told in a way that evokes memories bringing them to life. Together with my recollections are the reflective accounts from my journals and diaries that with time have allowed me to make sense of my experiences.

All biblical references are taken from the Kings James Version.

Preface

The primary purpose for writing my memoir is to share my experience of death and grieving in a way that will speak to other people's pain. My intention is to demonstrate how I grew out of adversity.

At the time of writing this book the entire world was gripped by the fear of a global pandemic called Covid-19. Many people lost their close relatives, friends, colleagues and neighbours. They lost their jobs and became financially insecure. There is considerable concern about its impact on the mental health of children and adults. We are grieving as a country for the people we know as well as those we do not know. Across the world there is global fear, anxiety and disquiet about the economy. We were all in the same boat. It feels as if fear had taken the place of hope as people became resigned to a siege called 'lockdown'. Governments across the world did not know how to respond to this unprecedented crisis. Millions of people contracted the virus. Many professionals, medical staff and care workers on the front line have lost their lives in the battle to contend with a faceless enemy. As we entered a phase where lockdown eased, there is and continues to be concern about its impact on the mental health of children and adults and the destruction it has left behind.

The process of grieving was hard. There are no words to explain the social isolation that confined us to our homes, not seeing or touching our loved ones and friends. I watched the devastation and felt helpless. My best way of dealing with this situation was to focus on completing this book. It was at this time that I began to think of how I could deal with what I describe as 'cabin fever.' I had started the process of writing my book, and was midway on my journey when the pandemic struck. I remembered that the story I was writing had the potential to inspire many people through this dismal period of suffering. There could no better time to give others a sense of hope. Covid-19 reminded me of the various types of losses I had suffered, the rollercoaster emotions I experienced and how I had grown out of them. The motivation to complete my book became urgent. I remembered that as far back as my childhood, I had suffered a significant loss that came like a whirlwind and washed over me like a giant wave. It felt as if the loss at that time was similar to Covid-19. It was the sudden nature of the death of my father that led to one of the biggest transitions in my life and heralded change of great proportions, namely emigration to the United Kingdom during the *Windrush* years.

There was a deeper loss I had suffered, yet the opportunity had not come to access the emotions that were buried deep within me. After all, it was a private loss that I had chosen not to expose. I had placed it in the background and simply made the best of a bad situation. Covid-19 had the effect of reminding me of the transient nature of life and it opened a door to positively reflect on how I had dealt with personal tragedy and trauma. At the time of this event I had no real tools to deal with the ravaging effects of bereavement, loss and grief. I became keenly aware that if I took this journey, opened myself to the world, my vulnerability could become another person's victory. This was the point at which I turned to my journals compiled over many years, and my Pandora's box. This treasure trove of memories was where I began my journey as I travelled back in time. It is my attempt to share my personal experiences and family relationships, as well as what I have learnt over the years that have been given to me to influence others. It is my hope that this book will bring a sense of encouragement and inspiration to those who read its pages.

Introduction

Nothing that God ever made is the same thing to more than one person. That is natural. There is no single face in nature, because every eye that looks upon it sees it from its own angle. So every man's spice box seasons his own food.

ZORA NEALE HURSTON, (1995)

There is a truth for all of us that is external and based on universal principles. Night follows day, the sun rises in the east and sets in the west. The law of gravity keeps us on the ground and oxygen is needed to replenish the air. The seasons follow each other with unfailing regularity, there are thorns on roses and the seed that dies in the ground gives way to new life in the spring. The child in the womb will be born. These things are immutable facts. We cannot change or add to them.

To everything there is a season and a time to every purpose under the heaven.

ECCLESIASTES 3:1 (HOLY BIBLE)

There is also a truth that is personal and related to our experiences and perception of the world and the seasons of our experiences. In this book, I present the 'Hard Truth' based on my experience of bereavement, grief and loss. Death is final and there is nothing that can change the fact that we are born to die. That is reality. This is my story of strength and survival after the deaths of my father, husband, mother and brother. Each loss was experienced differently and produced very different emotions. Yet, my story might have had a different outcome had it not been for earlier life experiences. The only certainty in life is that we are born to die. As is stated in the Bible:

> For we brought nothing into this world, and it is certain we can carry nothing out.
>
> 1 TIMOTHY 6:7 (HOLY BIBLE)

The best we can hope for is to leave an enduring legacy from which others can draw strength and comfort. One of my favourite actors, Denzel Washington, once said that he had never seen a U-Haul truck in a funeral procession. It is true that our material possessions are only as good as the time we are given in our lifespan to enjoy them.

There were countless occasions when I felt the urge to take the journey to write this book, but to do it; I had to open my 'Pandora's box'. On many occasions, I told myself that it would be a good thing to do, even if what was emitted from the box brought pain. Even so, I wanted others to benefit from my story. Yet, I procrastinated and delayed what is among one of the most important projects I have ever completed.

Life offers many opportunities to influence others and while I did not communicate my thoughts through the written word, I shared my story with many people as they struggled to overcome death, bereavement, loss, sadness and loneliness. The story I will tell encompasses all of these things as well as the victories, the hope and the success I achieved. I am engaging in this project because I want to inspire others to know that it is possible to become resilient by rising above adversity, and thus overcoming the disappointments we face and the troubles that threaten to destroy us.

During my lifetime, it has been encouraging to see how people found my words inspiring and would ask the inevitable question: 'So why haven't you written a book?'. It was a question that often confronted me; nevertheless, I managed to convince myself that my busy work life and schedule should come first; after all, it was my livelihood that was most important. I was also busy helping other people accomplish their dreams and thereby allowed my dream to fade into the background.

The natural lapse of time prevented me from writing my memoir, yet I realised that whenever I verbally communicated my story to others there was a quiver in my voice, and I was reliving the very experiences I tried so hard to shut away. The truth can be hard to process, but whether we accept it or not, truth does not change. Thus, I had to reach a point of acceptance before I appreciated that my story was the true legacy I will leave behind. I wanted to step off the proverbial merry-go-round, reflect and draw meaning from different elements of my life. Going back to a place of pain was paradoxical because I wanted to remember and I did not want to remember.

The other point worth mentioning as I introduce the thoughts in my book is that it was not until I began to think about what constitutes success that the realisation of my personal achievements against a backdrop of adversity became evident. In a real sense it was hidden beneath the rubble of loss, pain and anguish. It was sometimes disguised by putting on a brave face. Death is not all bad, therefore I had to search diligently for the good, and how it is possible to develop an overcoming spirit. This is a task that was demanding and time-consuming, it required motivation, visualization, and a huge emotional investment. My chief aim is to reflect and draw meaning from the various interconnected strands of my life.

My Pandora's box is a brown suitcase known as a valise that my husband had travelled with from Barbados to the United Kingdom with all of his worldly possessions in it. I was now using it to keep his memory alive. Although I did not see it on a daily basis, I knew that it was there behind the scenes. The need to open it came after I was invited to speak at a Metropolitan Police conference on September 17th 2018. This invitation came after I had attended a yearly remembrance ceremony. As I sat at a table, and the guests began to talk about their loved ones, I joined in the conversation. It was after I had spoken about my traumatic experience that Nicola, a police officer, invited me to give a keynote speech at a wellbeing event about my journey after the loss of my husband. As I prepared my speech, I instantly recognised the hard truth as being a point in my life when my wellbeing was suddenly stripped away. The disaster that had befallen me over forty-seven years ago was locked away in my Pandora's box and in the deepest recesses of my heart. It was a disaster that came one year after my marriage to Michael and one week before the birth of his son. Now here I was preparing to tell my story in a public arena.

In an effort to put the facts together, I instinctively went to my Pandora's box with fear and apprehension. I was afraid of the emotions it would call forth, but I knew that I had to confront the memories that I had hidden.

I was alone on the day I finally opened my Pandora's box with its secrets, whereupon I came face to face with the memories that challenged me to write this book. Instantaneously, I fell on my bed and sobbed. The tears came effortlessly, flowing down my cheeks; it was as if I was reliving a truth that occurred many years ago when I was given the tragic news of my husband's untimely demise.

The memories were vivid as I relived unspeakable grief and pain. The items I saw were not in any particular order; if anything, the contents seemed chaotic and as if it was done in a hurry and without thought, it was overflowing and overwhelming. In many respects this was a part of my life that had been compartmentalised and hidden for a more convenient time. The items were significant and each represented an important part of my life. Each item contributed to the story I am about to tell. There were many letters and cards from Mike (a reminder of our love for each other), newspaper articles (reporting the event), death certificate (finality) letters from various businesses, letters from the Metropolitan Police (information), bills and receipts (debt), Mike's spectacles (vision for what was to come), wedding photographs (lost love), bereavement cards (condolences), my son's first pair of shoes (milestones yet to come), coins (poverty or wealth) and much more. The case was full to capacity and the smell it emitted engulfed me. The picture that gripped my attention was a battered car, it was the police vehicle where my husband met his death. It was strange how I could not remember seeing this distinctive image before, yet here it was, stored as part of my memories. There was a smell that represented the passing of time; the keenness of smell was a strong indicator of time span. All of these things were functional at one time and told a story, but now they were historic artefacts of bygone times with significant meaning. It was at this point that I finally made the decision to commit to bringing my memories alive.

My book has the purpose of inspiring and helping anyone who has faced similar challenges and disappointments as myself to develop hope, and believe that even though they may go through hard experiences, it is possible to bounce back and find healing. It is my desire to connect with people on a human level, to meet them where they are, whether on the basis of their gender, social or cultural differences, religious, racial or ethnic background. It is my desire to reach out in a compassionate and empathic way to help others find healing in response to brokenness.

CHAPTER ONE

Childhood Memories

> I have one life and one chance to make it count for something ...
> My faith demands that I do whatever I can, wherever I am,
> whenever I can, for as long as I can with whatever I have to try to
> make a difference. .
>
> JIMMY CARTER PEACE PRIZE 2002

I believe that in this one life we have to live, a time will come when there will be no more death, tears, mourning or crying. We will be able to enjoy a vibrant life without disconnection from those we love and with those with whom we have lost a connection. In the meantime, we are walking by faith and not by sight.

I grew up for the first thirteen years of my life in Barbados. This is where I was born. I was fortunate to have six sisters and one brother and I enjoyed the closeness of family relationships. For me, being a part of a loving and caring family unit was one of the most important factors that contributed to my identity and sense of self. My parents were proud of their children and did whatever they could to make us feel happy and wanted. My siblings are Grace, Judy, Gozil, Pauline, Denise, Daryl (deceased) and Joy. I also had a brother called George, who died suddenly at the age of six. I have often wondered about him, but my mother said that he was a beautiful child. Because there were so many children there was a huge gap between the eldest and youngest. When my mother gave birth to her last child, my eldest sister gave birth to her first child.

I was encouraged to see family as a dependent and interdependent unit with many possibilities. It gave me a framework on which I was later able to build confidence in my ability to accomplish many goals.

1

Within my family, we relied on each other for support. My parents were firm believers in presenting an image of unity to the world. They were industrious and hardworking people who believed in the work ethic. They were well-intentioned people.

To a greater extent, my childhood was a happy and carefree one. I remember spending days at the seaside bathing in the blue sea, the limitless sun, lying on the beach, walking on the soft brown sand, going for picnics and collecting seashells. I enjoyed the company of children and adults. I also remember that children were not allowed to actively join in adult conversations. There was a distinct line that children could not cross. It was a time when I simply relished life. It was a time of innocence and a time of freedom. It was a time of scarcity and a time of abundant love. I knew it and I felt it. There was no fear of leaving doors open; there was a sense of safety and trust between children and adults.

I remember gazing at the stars and the moon and wondering about their constellation. I wondered who put them in place and about the brightness of the moon as it lit up the streets when nightfall came. The grasshoppers buzzed as daylight evaporated when suddenly, and without warning, darkness fell. I recall the hawkers along the road selling all sorts of food and merchandise. Their trays were filled with nuts and confectionery. They did not have shops; thus, the sidewalks were a perfect way to make a living. The smell of the fish along the main streets and fishermen walking the streets selling the local fish as they caught them was a familiar sight, and a custom I have long since remembered. I even remember the smell of the streets as the rain hit the hot tarmac. The smells and sounds of the busy streets and the markets are consciously integrated as anchors in my mind.

Among my memories is waking as first light broke and walking to the beach to bathe in the expansive sea. This was something that families did together and it helped us to enjoy nature as a small community. I recall that one morning a cousin pushed my head under the water and held it there for several seconds. After my breath hit the air, I was fluttering like a bird. This led to a fear of swimming, a skill that I have never quite conquered. Before going to school, we had to complete chores around the house. There was organisation and we knew the boundaries and the rules.

Playing simple games with friends and going on picnics on bank holidays were common activities that occupied my time as a child. We played childish games like hopscotch, and riddles with the girl who lived opposite but who was not allowed to play with other children in the street. It was an oddity because others said that her mother had strange practices going on in her house. They did not have visitors and her mother never spoke to anyone. We often wondered what was going on behind closed doors.

Christmas was a busy and exciting time of the year as preparations were made to refurbish the home. New curtains draped the windows, beds were overturned and the house was subjected to a cleaning like never before. Christmas Day was eagerly anticipated because we received treats that were not given throughout the year. At Christmas time, food was plentiful and there were generous helpings for everyone. Mama would bake her famous coconut sweetbread and Christmas cake. I never knew which one to eat first as they were both delicious. Everyone was allowed to eat to their heart's content.

Even though my parents did not have an abundance of money they made an effort to give us whatever was within their means but without indulgence. This is how I learnt the concept of delayed gratification and how to save for the things I wanted. It was tantalizing window-shopping and seeing the toys my parents could not afford. It was not only that the things I saw in the window of a big department store called Cave Shepherd were expensive, but in my world, the presentation of the items represented an extravagant lifestyle. So, I enjoyed looking at them but walked away knowing that those things did not belong in my world. I recall the big pink fluffy storks in the shop window suggesting that babies came from storks. The stark reality, however, was that once babies were born parents in the community where we lived could not afford the things that came with storks. It was hard for most parents who tried to make ends meet. It was a strange juxtaposition, but I have since wondered if the idea of the stork placed a fantasy in people's minds. The stork was a fantasy and poverty were the reality. But this is the way it was.

My parents' approach to gift-giving struck a balance between abject poverty and living just above the breadline. In other words, we did not need to have the best outfit but just enough to make us feel happy and not to be set apart from other children. So it was, that my mother would make clothes and recreate clothes that fitted the next child down the line. Her industrious way of thinking and ingenuity created the illusion of affordability. When my dad came home with a loaf of bread and a tin of corned beef, he would give us thick slices, but Mama would say cut it thinner, she knew that there were many mouths to feed and would take care to make the food go further.

One of the special events I recall was walking to the garrison after the Christmas service where many families gathered to hear the band play and see the decorations along Broad Street throughout the festive season. One of life's luxuries was the music I listened to on the Barbados radio Rediffusion. My father loved classical music. Indeed, I gained a love for classical music and jazz during my most formative years. It was a grand time.

Cricket was the national sport played at the famous Kensington Oval cricket ground a stone's throw from the local area where I grew up. But any field was a site for cricket. Within my heritage as a Barbadian is the famous cricketer Sir Gary Sobers. He became a national hero and rose to great heights and many children aspired to be like him.

We were not rich by any stretch of the imagination, life was not a rose garden, and we did not wear rose-tinted glasses. Having material possessions was not as important as the values we were taught. Instead, we were taught about the importance of caring for others, of family life and togetherness created through mutual aid and sharing.

My mother cherished the notion that there should always be something in the food cupboard for the wayfaring stranger. Her gift at making traditional Barbadian cuisine was always relished and was a delight. I first learnt to cook soup when I was around eleven years old. I loved being in the kitchen with Mama. She was a master in the art of traditional Barbadian dishes.

Looking back, I have come to realise that I was taught values that were deeply embedded in the concept of family and within the cultural life of the community where I was raised. These values were the real lenses through which my parents saw the world. A value that became a guiding principle and was firmly planted in my mind is the golden rule: *A person must do to others, as they would want others to do to them*. My parents taught me that children had to respect their elders and show deference to them. Adults were never to be addressed by their first names but were to be called 'aunty' and 'uncle'. In the absence of these titles, adults were referred to as Sir, Miss or Mrs. Simple words such as 'please', 'thank you', 'excuse me', 'speak when you are spoken to', 'do not interrupt adults when they are speaking' were religiously taught and thus embedded in my consciousness. These little things made all the difference to the relationship children developed with adults and how children were disciplined. Values such as honesty and truth-telling were consciously embedded in my mind. Many of the values I was taught also created the feeling that I always needed to please others and always needed to give of myself.

Members of the community and people with authority had the blessing of parents to correct children and to set them on the right path. At times the punishment teachers gave were harsh and insensitive, but it was a cultural value led by the wisdom of elders and those who purported to know what was best for children. In effect, it was the community that parented children because parenting was not seen as a task allotted only to birth parents, but to everyone who came into contact with children. In today's society, we have come a long way from these ideals and it has had consequences for our offspring.

I grew up with the idea that everyone in the family had to play their role and take their responsibility. Children watched, learnt and then performed tasks. Therefore, at an early age, I learnt valuable life skills, all of which were practical and intended to prepare me for adulthood. Being part of a big family meant that older siblings were given greater responsibility and, in some respects, did some of the parenting. It was a method of survival and it helped to build resilience and strength of character in me, even though I did not know it at the time. It introduced into my unconscious mind that caring for others was not only a responsibility but also a duty. To act in this way instilled a source of pride within the traditions and values that were laid down and spelt out for children.

Social support came from the small community where I was raised. Families often relied on extended relatives and friends to help with children when they could not cope financially. In some cases, it was not shameful for grandparents to take over the care of the first-born child. It was a cultural tradition for extended family members and godparents to step in and help struggling parents. The nature of kinship bonds kept people and communities closely knitted together with the proverbial saying 'It takes a village to raise a child'.

Generally, though, grandmothers played a pivotal role in caring for children, they were seen as matriarchs with the responsibility for supporting, guiding and taking over the care of their grandchildren. It was a cultural custom and an unspoken responsibility. Although my grandmother did not look after me, I visited her frequently and had a positive relationship with her. She had many sons; some of them lived abroad and sent her money and gifts for the children they had left behind in her care. She appeared to me to be rich because she lived in a good-sized house, always had food and at Christmas she had a hugely decorated Christmas tree accompanied by an array of gifts.

My grandmother was elderly yet agile. Nevertheless, she became my first encounter with death. Adults did not speak to children about death or the reasons for it, therefore she faded away and was no longer around or spoken about. What I can recall about my paternal grandmother was that she had long flowing hair, she was a good cook, would hide the 'coconut bread' (a Barbadian delicacy) under her bed when we visited and she used something called 'snuff'. She kept the snuff in a small box. She would insert it into her nostrils and then sneeze several times. I would watch her and wonder why she did it and what pleasure she gained from it. I now know that it was a drug addiction. We may think that in today's world these types of addictions are new, but as Solomon, the wisest man who ever lived, stated, 'There is nothing new under the sun'. Ecclesiastes 1:9 (Holy Bible)

The loss of my grandmother removed a form of support even if it was only going to visit her. Nevertheless, in reflecting I understand that the kinship network had a utilitarian function and it worked well for struggling families. It was this thinking that led my father to take one of my sisters to her godmother without warning. As he prepared to leave, she clung to him and cried uncontrollably, so much that he dared not leave her behind. This would have been a great loss to our family had it not been for her vehement and boisterous protestation.

Personal Reflections

Childhood memories are extremely important because they provide the baseline for all future life experiences. They provide a guideline for how we interpret the world, our relationships and the memories we build on a daily basis. Helping children to feel a sense of security does not only mean being able to give them the finer things in life. It means combining protection and the prevention of harm. Children feel happy and contented when they are loved, well connected, and disciplined even though they may live with poverty and hardship. Childhood poverty does not determine a person's happiness, character or his/her capability to make the most of his/her life. It is rather the simple things in life that contribute to a child's happiness. Today, children are living in a complex world with gadgets that draw them away from communicating in ways that would help them to build positive and fruitful relationships. They are attached to things rather than people. Happiness does not depend on material things, but on a person's state of mind and belief system. Contentment also brings great gain. One of the childhood memories that troubled me for many years was growing up in poverty, which had an impact on the way I began to think and feel about myself. It is only with hindsight that I realise that happiness was of greater importance.

The story of childhood poverty is one of the memories that had an impact on me and which was one of my hard truths. It determined where I lived, the school I attended, and to a greater extent, the opportunities I was given. As a child, I grew up in a community where all families suffered the same fate. They were destined to live a life of nothingness as the revolving doors of poverty opened up and engulfed them. It was as if there was no way out. Yet, I did not see it as happening to them, but as happening to me and my family. The only way to survive was for families to share the little they had or to be content with their lot in life. The problem is that poverty can lead to apathy and a sense of hopelessness and inertia. For years I lived with the shame of admitting to myself and certainly to others, that I came from a poor family and an improvised community where there were few resources. As I reflect on the past, I know that the future was bleak except that the hand of fate turned loss into gain and poverty into opportunity. The destination for which I was headed changed, giving me the chance that I would not have had if my mother had not made a great sacrifice. Cusk (2001) point to several values that a mother acquires. Mama had three of them, namely virtue, self-sacrifice and love.

When my grandson was four years old, I was travelling with him to one of his swimming lessons. It is an activity that he loves and enjoys. As we were driving my son played a song on a CD called 'Happy' by Pharrell Williams. My grandson immediately said, 'I love that song'. I wondered what made him feel that way. I concluded that as a child he connected the words with his feelings. It was a feeling of joyfulness and contentment in that time and space. On another occasion when he was visiting me, we had a long debate about animals. He was seven years old and I was amazed at the ideas he could express. At the end of this intriguing conversation he said, 'I want to be a Marine Conservationist'. It reminded me that this was not something I could say at the age of seven. Yet, I am fortunate to have had many happy memories of my childhood. Poverty and happiness were strangely combined during my most impressionable years and gave me an appreciation of both in later life.

My Early Education

I began my education in earnest at the age of five years old. This was the established custom in Barbados. Before this time children remained at home. The stimulation I received came from playing games with my siblings and other children in the community. Thus, play activities were the foundation for learning during the early years of my development. There were so many children for Mama to look after that it must have come as a relief for us to spend part of our day outside the home, and in an educational establishment.

On my very first day at school, I clearly remember that I was standing in line with my peers and it was in that line that I had a rude awakening and an introduction to the male anatomy. A boy standing next to me took out his private part and bravely waved it around. I yelled at the top of my voice in fear, as I had never seen what boys looked like underneath their clothing. He was immediately dragged out of the line by a teacher and was chastised with a strap. Today I know that what that teacher did was excessive punishment, it was not positive discipline that would help the child to learn about the inappropriateness of his behaviour. Teachers had an undisputed authority to discipline children, and this was usually with the strap or a cane or forcing the child to stand in a corner with their hands outstretched in the air for long periods. I cannot remember ever having any more interactions with that boy, but I remember feeling vindicated. Consequently, that was my introduction to formal education and for that matter an untimely introduction to authority.

My early education continued without event or interruption and I eventually graduated to secondary school. I took the 11+ examinations but failed them. This was the first time when I felt what failure looked and felt like. There were three elite schools in Barbados, one called Queen's College for girls, and two for boys called Harrison College and Combermere. These schools were reserved for children of academic promise, the brightest and the best. They were usually white children and children from middle-class black families. Bright children from poor families also gained entry to these schools. Those who did not achieve high results, but did reasonably well, were given entry to the next schools in line. The uniforms these children wore were distinctive and set them apart from other children, or that was my perception. Just wearing the uniform said something about their status. I now know that they were no better than myself but it was my perception and what I felt. My thinking was somewhat misguided, but it reflected my reality. Children like me who did not make the grade were relegated to ordinary schools. I attended St Leonard's Secondary School until I was thirteen years old. This too reinforced my sense of under-achievement. It is strange, but the only real memory I have of my early education is writing essays and domestic science. I was good at making cakes and I did it with pride. It gave me contentment to share the art of cooking with family and friends.

I now know that as a result of the limitations of my early and later education I lacked self-confidence. My saving grace was that I was very bold and would always put my best foot forward, acting as if I knew what I did not know. At times when I felt inwardly afraid, I pretended that I had the capability and would go away and find the answers to the things I did not know. This was similar to what my parents did because they also gave the appearance of better things, better ways of knowing, and acting in certain ways even if they were living in dire situations. In looking back, it feels as if I had a gift that had not been developed due ostensibly to my positioning in life and the class into which I was born, but it also felt as if by some strange benevolence I was able to rise above them and become successful in later life.

Personal Reflections

Our earliest learning comes through stimulation, and transmission of ideas from significant others and then teachers. During a child's early education there are many hurdles to overcome. Poverty is one of the factors that can have a detrimental impact on a child's education, on confidence building and the realisation of their true potential. It is a task that many parents and caregivers often neglect, particularly when they rely solely on educators to meet their children's educational needs. During the era when I was growing up, playing was not considered to be part of a child's formal education, but today I know that this thinking was incorrect. Play has a vital role in stimulating a child's mind, giving them the ability to become creative and abstract thinkers. Play is usually used as a form of therapy for children who have suffered significant forms of abuse and loss because it helps them to communicate on another level using the language of play.

One of the things I have learnt, as a lecturer, is that when learners in any age category doubt that they can learn, then failure is almost certain. It is the way we think and what we do with the tools and the gifts we have at our disposal that make the difference. I have worked with many adult learners who came into my classes saying that they could not achieve. They doubted themselves, leading them to self-sabotage. This made it harder for them to achieve higher grades. I have also seen that with the right type of support and with confidence-building, students can graduate and become successful contrary to low expectations, whether self-imposed or imposed by others. While others may place limitations on us as children or as adults, we should not allow those limitations to stop us from reaching our goals. We should never draw a line in the sand and say this is what I am capable of achieving. It is through the very act of drawing the line in the sand that we develop self-limiting beliefs. The nature/nurture debate has questioned whether we become who we are as a result of the environment we inhabit or the genes we inherit. To some extent there is truth in both perspectives.

Daddy & Mama

CHAPTER TWO

Memories of my Father

And God shall wipe away all tears from their eyes; and there shall be no more death, neither sorrow, nor crying, neither shall there be any more pain: for the former things are passed away.

REVELATION 21:4 (HOLY BIBLE)

My father was a bespoke tailor and he worked on a freelance basis for a prestigious company called CB Rice to produce some of the most fashionable suits of his day. He was clever and he possessed a unique skill. In actuality he was self-employed within this company. However, his trade often meant that people would not pay the price when the product was completed, therefore he struggled to make ends meet and to be the breadwinner. To be the breadwinner said something about his pride and male ego. Within my culture men had the responsibility of providing for their family. It was a responsibility my dad took seriously. Despite his best intentions at times, he was overtaken by discouragement, felt demoralised and turned to alcohol when the funds were not forthcoming. I cannot say when he developed this habit but I know that alcohol consumption was a national pastime. I recall that when I was twelve years old, I saw Daddy as he walked down the street trying to hold his head high but walking in a zigzag fashion. My sister jokingly said: 'He was blind drunk but he still kept his head high.'

It was easy to get access to rum in Barbados; we had it in abundance, firstly because sugar cane was plentiful and was an exportable product that brought economic gain. Indeed, the sugar cane industry was built on slave labour. The plantation masters during a period of colonialism thrived on the production of sugar, rum and their derivatives. Second, many people sold rum – indeed one of my uncles owned a liquor shop where men would frequently congregate at the end of the working day or even through the day. When my father was discouraged, he would go to his brother's liquor shop before returning home. It was well positioned in his path to our home and was a temptation he could not resist.

The hard truth at this point in my life was the fact that alcohol had a devastating impact on his health and the wellbeing of his family but it was not talked about or mentioned in any way. I believe that it was accepted as a fact of life. This was what people did, how they spent their time and lived their lives. Thus, the image that my dad tried to portray to the outside world was far from the truth on the inside because alcohol consumption affected the way he related to my mother. It had a devastating impact on how he communicated, expressed his frustration, and consequently his temperament and his moods. On the days when Daddy did not drink alcohol, he was a good father, he cared about his children, but when he drank it took hold of his mind and changed his character.

There was a deeper truth that as a child I did not see or understand about my dad. It was that his second child, George, whom he adored, died suddenly at the age of six. I did not meet George, but by all accounts, he was a beautiful child. It was believed that he had diphtheria but I will never know the true reason for his passing, as my parents did not speak of him. My parents carried this grief and mourned silently, I believe, from the depths of their hearts. It was an enormous weight to carry without support, and without access to counselling, the door to healing was closed and they were both caught up in the vortex of pain, suffering and anguish. However, it could have been the prime reason why my dad turned to alcohol for comfort, while my mother turned to God for the same comfort. They had two different coping mechanisms and it took them down different paths.

My father had great vision and he wanted the best for his children, but for whatever reason he did not have the tools to deal with the corrosive effects of a habit he had developed. As a tailor he was fastidious and presentation meant everything to him. He counselled his children about the way they should look, by telling them that if they only had one pair of shoes, they should be polished so brightly that a person could see the image of their face mirrored in them. He kept a watchful eye over his daughters and protected them from the boys in the local neighbourhood. He had a deep belief in the concept of self-pride and held fast to the notion that self-image spoke volumes about one's character. This was all about mirror image and prestige and deeply held values.

From a religious point of view, my dad was raised in the Anglican Church, but as an adult he made his choices, which included abandoning any allegiance to his faith. Nevertheless, he supported his children and would come to our church when there were special programmes where we were performing. It was in her later years that Mama became a Seventh Day Adventist. It was through diligent study of the Bible that she gained a better understanding of the Sabbath and Bible prophesies.

It was not until many years later when one of my aunts was dying of cancer that one of my sisters and I visited her at her home in Canada. As we talked and called forth memories of family life and the good old days, to my dismay, she revealed a dislike for my dad. She openly admitted that she felt that he harboured feelings of superiority. Apparently, it was the way he walked and held his head high that made her feel that he felt himself to be better than others. This was a painful moment for me. She knew that behind closed doors, we lived in poverty, but from the outside, it did not appear that way to onlookers. Nevertheless, he gave the impression that all was well in our household. My view is that a person does not have to be rich to subscribe to values of personhood or to aim for higher goals. After all, it is by setting high standards that we are able to aspire to greater heights.

During the early 1950s and well into the 1960s the British government were seeking to rebuild their country following the Second World

War. Barbados was a part of the Commonwealth due to colonialism. We had a history of enslavement and were tethered to what was known as the mother country. British government officials came to Barbados in search of people who wanted to train and work in various professions from nursing to the transportation systems and other developing industries. Some of the early immigrants were professionally qualified but could not secure employment in white collar jobs. In order to survive they were forced to work in dirty and low paid jobs. Nurses were desperately needed to re-establish the National Health Service (NHS). It was a system that was under threat. It was during this time that my father had the vision to send his first daughter to Britain to be trained as a nurse. His intention was to provide a way of escape and a new life for his family. He had tried over and over again to emigrate under this plan but his every attempt to find a way to support his family was thwarted. He had twelve siblings, most of whom were brothers. They were the Oxley family. Many of his brothers succeeded where he had failed. My dad's application was denied on several occasions because he was told that there were too many Oxley boys applying to leave the island. It was on this assumption that he was rejected. This rejection intensified his frustration and led to further disillusionment and disappointment and a sense of failure.

During 1958, my parents prepared to send their first daughter, who was eighteen years old, to Hampshire, England, to study nursing after she passed the examination that gave entry to this programme. In actuality, she preferred to go to America or Canada because both were the countries where her cousins were allocated, but this was not to be her fate. For reasons known only to God, she was sent to England, a country we knew nothing about and with which there was no personal association. Popular myths existed that the streets of England were paved with gold. In other words, people would become rich quickly. Thus, my parents had an expectation that she would complete her training, earn money and help those of us that remained behind. As many parents left their children behind with family and friends, they held on to the common myth that they would work and earn sufficient funds to return to the island within five years. This was a hope that did not materialise. This was an aspiration that became a common theme associated with emigration and how families looked for opportunities to survive.

My father made a suit out of quality woven fabric for my sister to wear and we waved her goodbye from the shores of Bridgetown, Barbados. The reality was that as she entered the ship, we had no conception of where she was going, how long she would be away or if we would see her again. This was the first loss in my family and one that would lead to deep resentment on my sister's part. She felt as if she was being hurled out of the family to fend for herself. It was a swift loss that none of us truly understood. Her departure left my parents with seven children – six girls and one boy. I was placed sixth of the siblings. I guess it was a strategic position because I had a central role to play in my family later on in life.

After my eldest sister gave birth to her first child, my parents sent their second daughter to assist her. With the two eldest children gone, our parents had to cope with the departure of two children simultaneously. In many ways the departure of both siblings was a loss for the entire family. They were not moving to another part of the island but to another country that we knew very little about.

I had just turned twelve years old when my dad arrived home late one Friday evening feeling exceedingly ill. He was in excruciating pain and it took him to his bed. His discomfort began at work and his colleagues brought him home. It was clear that his pain was intolerable. The erect position that he took when walking down the avenue was no longer visible. This was unusual for my dad because I had never witnessed him in this or any other condition that slightly resembled an illness. This incident was unusual and strangely frightening because of its suddenness and severity. He was vomiting uncontrollably and it was tainted with blood. We did not know the extent of his illness, but it appeared to be serious.

My mother [Mama] was a woman of action and she spared no time in fixing him some home remedies, none of which worked or lessened his pain. His discomfort continued throughout the night and did not subside. Illness of such magnitude has an impact on family life particularly when it is the main person with the responsibility for a family's survival and safety. Thus it was that on the following day my mother had no alternative but to seek medical intervention. The Queen Elizabeth Hospital was some distance from our home; therefore, I cannot recall how she managed to get him there, but she did. The waiting time was long, as we sat around anxiously waiting for him to receive medical attention. Eventually, he was admitted. We all hoped that Daddy would receive the attention he needed and would be back home imminently. This was not to be the case, as he remained in the QEH over the weekend. It was a tense time for my family. Along with Mama, I visited Daddy on the Sunday afternoon of that weekend, and saw him writhing in agony. He was delirious. His pain was unquestionable, but what I saw was frightening as he struggled to dislodge the various wires that were strapped to his body. He appeared to have great strength as he groaned like a woman in travail; he was contorted as he twisted and turned his body to set himself free of the contraptions and intravenous tubes that bound him to the bed. He shouted and his eyes were like great balls of fire. This was my first observation of what a person can go through when they are delirious and nearing the end of their life. It was frightening to observe it. Yet, I did not sense that death was near. I still hoped that his recovery would be swift.

Death and Mourning

The weekend had just ended and we were about to start a new week. It was a day in November 1962. All of the children were getting ready for school when we heard a high-pitched voice approaching our house. It was the familiar voice of my father's niece, the same person who had pushed my head under the water in the sea. She was a highly-strung and insensitive woman. We thought that there was something not quite right about her, but it might have been that her mental state was unbalanced. She worked at the hospital and got the first news that daddy had died. As she approached the house my mother was given the hard truth. It was the unpalatable news that stunned us to the core and rooted each one of us to the spot where we were standing. She shouted, Sissy! Sissy! (my mother's nickname) Phony (my father's abbreviated name for Alphonzo) is dead! My father died at the age of forty-nine as a result of pancreatic cancer, but for many years I carried around the belief that it was a stomach ulcer. Feelings of shock and disbelief were the central emotion at play.

The day that Daddy was suddenly taken away from our midst turned out to be the worst day of our lives. Each eye was filled with tears; there were screams, dismay and even mayhem as we tried to process what had happened. Mama said that on one of her visits to see him, he had made peace with God and asked for forgiveness. The truth of what he did or did not do remained with Mama and became part of her private ruminations. All I knew was that on hearing the news Mama drew each of her children to herself, as a chicken would draw her chicks under her wings. She looked up to heaven and prayed to God for protection and for his providence in making the next step. Protection and providence appeared to be her most urgent need at that time.

Immediately after the passing of my father, I had mixed feelings because as a child I did not truly understand what his sudden departure would mean for my family and myself. I saw alcohol as the chief reason for his demise. I knew that when he was intoxicated, he would abuse my mother. In many ways, I saw his departure as an end to my mother's suffering. I had tried on many occasions to intervene on Mama's behalf and it earned me the displeasure of my father. Hence, when he passed away, I felt relief, and I blamed him for many things including leaving us destitute. The true significance of his passing was only to be revealed as time passed, and as I came to grips with and owned up to my grief.

The Funeral

As I recall, in the culture where I grew up, death was treated with solemnity. It was a custom for people from the community to gather around and express their sympathy and mourn with the bereaved. It was considered to be comforting for friends to openly express their grief and sympathise with the family in their calamity. With so many children to take care of, people wondered what would happen to us. Some even came to the conclusion that as we were a female-dominated family, pregnancy would be the next natural step.

There was a custom to bring the body of the deceased to the family home before the church service and interment. On the day of the funeral, Daddy was brought to our home and people came from near and far to pay their last respects and say goodbye. My dad was buried but there was no budget for a headstone. It was during my research for this book that I read letters that my mother had kept. I learnt that after arriving in England and settling in a job, she had sent money to a friend to erect a headstone in his memory. Mama was a private person – she did not speak openly about Daddy, but she sat quietly, and in her heart, she remembered him.

Death brings closure and ending, but my true mourning and closure did not take place until several years later when I was in my late teens. By this time, I had joined my mother and siblings who were resident in England. I was sitting in church and as the final hymn was sung, the words of a hymn that was sung at his funeral reverberated in my ears and my head. It brought back a powerful evocation of memories that I had fought hard to put behind me. In an instant, I was transported back to the day of my dad's funeral and this hymn became the harbinger of that ill-fated day when the news suddenly came. It was not anticipated, but sudden and traumatic. It was only at this time that

I realised that my dad's sudden passing was tragic and, in many respects, painful. In my mind's eye it brought the memories flooding back. I needed to forgive myself as much as I needed to forgive my dad. I could barely sing the lyrics of that well-known hymn that we sang as he was laid to rest. The hymn was 'Abide with Me'. The words were:

Abide with me fast falls the eventide;
The darkness deepens Lord with me abide;
When other helpers fade and comforts flee;
Help, of the helpless oh, abide with me.
Swift to its close ebbs out life's little day;
Earth's joys grow dim; its glories pass away;
Change and decay in all around I see;
Oh, Thou who changes not abide with me.
I fear no foe, with Thee at hand to bless;
Ills have no weight, and tears no bitterness,
Where is death's sting?
Where, grave, they victory?
I triumph still if thou abide with me.
Hold Thou They cross before my closing eyes;
Shine through the gloom and point me to the skies;
Heaven's morning breaks, and earth's vain shadows flee;
In life, in death, O Lord, abide with me.

HENRY FRANCIS LYTE

Personal Reflections

Life is not a bed of roses. There are different challenges in our lives that we must come to terms with, and we must learn how to navigate the twists and turns on life's path. The hardest truth for me was to accept the truth about my dad. I lived in denial for many years refusing to accept that my dad was an alcoholic and that I had lived with domestic abuse. It took many years to acknowledge its profound affect and its damaging results. Hence, I hid it and pretended that all was well. I found it difficult to disclose the impact it had on the entire family. I had personal knowledge of the impact of alcoholism, thus I had made a decision to be an abstainer as a result of what I had observed during my childhood. Today as a result of my training, I know that children living in families where there is alcoholism and domestic abuse are at risk. I understand the blight that it had on my life. What saved my siblings and me was the protection that Mama gave us. She created an alternative narrative that positively challenged the negative one in its tracks.

When I think about the place where I was born, it seemed like an idyllic place to begin life, and it was, but when I think of the environment and the circumstances of my life, I know that I was not born with a silver spoon in my mouth. If anything, it was quite the reverse. I was born into poverty and at a disadvantage and it was not of my doing, it was just a fact of life. There was a lot of hardship not just for my family but for many other families. It was one of the life experiences that I only truly understood when I became an adult. Moreover, it was only when I became a social worker and saw the struggles and challenges that children and their families faced that I understood what it meant to escape a life of destruction. I escaped it by holding my head high like my dad and refusing to accept defeat. I can now accept that my dad also influenced my life as I know it today. All was not lost.

As hard as it was to accept, it was not at the time of the funeral but at the time when I heard the song. It was at that time that a connection was made in my brain, it was transferred to my vision. I could see the coffin in the front room and I could see my dad as he lay peacefully. His countenance had changed and he was at peace. It was then that I finally came to grips with my childhood loss. This was the time when I cried bitterly for my dad. It was as if my grief was suspended in mid-air for a time such as this.

Childhood grief is no different from the grief that adults face, but it is processed differently. Facing the death of a parent during childhood leaves unanswered questions that need to be explained sympathetically to help children understand that it was not their fault. The circumstances under which the grief occurred, as well as the support they are given, undoubtedly have a unique bearing on how children interpret this traumatic life experience. It was a good thing that Mama allowed me to see my dad before he was laid to rest. This action stopped me developing fears of where he had gone. I knew that he had died and would not return to our family.

One of the factors that stopped the grieving process for me was the fact that I thought it was my father's addiction to alcohol that brought about his demise. While alcohol might have been a contributory factor, it was not the complete truth as there were other factors such as stress and a family history of cancer that increased his propensity to inherit that disease. He had also suffered the deep loss of his son and the trauma of it led to high stress and thereby alcohol provided a route of escapism. If stress cannot be resolved through natural methods, or if there is a lack of personal and community resources, people resort to other harmful measures to reduce the tension caused by stress. These were the factors that eluded me as a child. In my reflections, I now understand that I could only rely on the immediacy of my limited understanding and observations at the time. I did not see the bigger picture; neither could I see the world through my father's lenses. For him, the world must have appeared like an unkind place.

Adults must recognise the need to talk to children and help them process their feelings of grief as soon as is practicable. My mother hardly had time to process her own grief let alone that of her children. Her focus was on survival. Grief during childhood can be difficult to understand and even harder to explain if it becomes complicated. It can lead to depression and negative thought processes. The loss I suffered during my childhood opened the door to lack of self-confidence and self-esteem.

A significant feature of bereavement during childhood is the inability to think logically. Therefore, children must depend on adults to help them with their grief and sense of bewilderment. This requires explanations in ways that children can understand. Unfortunately, I was growing up at a time when parents did not speak openly about their grief, much less explain such a bewildering experience to children.

Cairns and Fursland (2008) suggest that there are two ways in which a child can be traumatised and their considerations can be easily applied to separation and loss. The first consideration is developmental trauma where they argue that 'the brain is compromised with a range of effects on their development'. The second consideration is emotional trauma which affects a child's ability to regulate and tolerate stress. If death occurs as in my case when I was old enough to have some understanding, even if limited, it helps to regulate the stress. On the other hand, where there is 'overwhelming stress or horror it leads to extreme stress which can injure the brain and impact the child's ability to regulate'. Further, they state that the accumulation of stress during childhood makes all other lifetime traumas difficult to comprehend, consequently making them more difficult to overcome.

Trauma never goes away because it is painful and agonising. However, we can learn how to cope with the intense emotions that result in the aftermath of an incident that leads to stress and overwhelm. For example, in my work with a client called Delores, it became evident that after having suffered abuse during childhood she was traumatised. She spent the remainder of her childhood and adolescent years in foster care. She was unable to form a secure attachment with her caregivers. Consequently, she was unable to regulate her behaviour. As an adult she is still mentally affected by the scars of her early life experiences. Helping Delores to find the internal mechanisms to cope with her past experiences was at the very centre of her healing. The tipping point is how a trusting relationship is restored.

CHAPTER THREE

Memories of my Mother

We called our mother Mama. She was one of three girls born to her parents. She was born on 18 February 1917. She was the eldest of the girls and had a special place in her grandfather's heart. My maternal grandmother died when my mother was just eighteen, leaving her with the responsibility of caring for two younger sisters. Before my grandmother died, she disclosed to my mother that her grandfather had left her an inheritance. This inheritance was his house. Her father sought to disinherit my mother from this gift. My mother was a very determined woman with an intrepid spirit and when he refused to abide by my grandfather's wishes she took him to court and to his utter dismay won her case. This was a battle that caused her father and sisters to cut off all communication with her and one that grieved my mother into her old age. What it meant was that my mother lost all contact with her father and siblings. Thus, I did not know my maternal grandfather or my aunts; neither did I have any interactions with them. This branch of my family was cut off like a branch is cut off from its roots.

My parents met shortly after Mama's estrangement from her family. They lived in different parts of the island but my mother attended what they called High Church (Church of England). Dancing was allowed in that denomination. It was at a party that they met, courted and were married. After marrying him Mama used her inheritance to purchase a family home near to the location where my father's parents were living. This was the vicinity in which I grew up.

Mama had suffered the loss of her mother, father and siblings during a critical period in her life, yet she was able to overcome it and raise her children single-handedly. I wondered about her secret and discovered that she had lived a life of faith and a rich spiritual life of giving and sacrifice. I listened with disbelief and utter amazement, as my mother unfolded the story of her past family conflict and isolation to me. I was astonished at her resilience and fortitude even as a young woman. It made me take a long hard look at my struggles and myself, and in looking I saw some of the characteristics of my mum reflected in my life. I observed that one of her qualities was persistence – she was, as one of my friends said, 'a tough cookie'. She did not give up easily and I learnt by osmosis how to be brave and unafraid. With her strong belief that with God all things are possible she worked hard to reverse the tide of misfortune. She portrayed an image of being invincible and it was an image I adopted. When I often went to her with problems her first words would be *'let us pray'*. She used prayer as her ammunition and gateway to God.

Mama was a housewife and a seamstress. She worked at home making mattress covers for a local businessman. She also made clothing created from her own patterns. She spoke with a distinctive 'Bajan' accent and frequently used colloquial language that had profound meaning. She had excellent communication skills. I know this because of her letters and the comments she penned in her Bible. She underlined verses and committed them to memory so that she had a verse to share with others for every occasion and season of their lives.

As a housewife, my mother's main role was to look after the home and her children. During the era when my mother was growing up, girls and boys were perceived in different ways and were ultimately assigned gender-specific roles. The idea that girls were better suited to domestic roles was passed down through the generations. So it was that as I was growing up it was an expectation that girls would learn life skills. I recall being sent to a dressmaker to learn a craft called 'smocking', which is a type of embroidery used on bodices. It was a creative art form that increased the attractiveness of a dress. Most girls learnt smocking or a similar craft to prepare them for homely duties.

Although my mother had a desire to become a teacher, this was a dream that did not materialise for a number of reasons. The role she played in the home was a significant one. But in reality, it was a male-dominated society and women were not given the same opportunities to work outside the home or to become as successful as men. They were encouraged to focus on developing life skills that were fitted to the task of child-rearing. Therefore, she worked at home as a seamstress while caring for her children. It was the best and most important role she could have played at that time.

Mama was singularly responsible for the religious affiliation we had as a family with the church we attended every Sunday and she was the spiritual centre of our family. She was converted to the Christian faith when a woman stood outside her door in the early hours of the morning and shared Bible texts and songs. She incessantly repeated the words, 'If anyone in the hearing of my voice would like to know more come to the First Baptist Church'. It turned out that while my dad would urge her to come away from the window, her interest was intensified and she wanted to hear and know more.

The decision she made to join forces with the local community church changed the course of our lives. There were many charitable acts of kindness and benevolence given by church members from which we greatly benefited. The pastor was an American and he frequently brought huge boxes of clothing and other gifts for church members. My siblings and I had access to these gifts that often came when we were in need. In later life, I remembered his actions and it taught me the act of gratitude and giving to those who are less fortunate than myself.

After my mother was converted to the Christian faith, church life became a fundamental part of our lives. We were often asked to sing and perform in small plays and recite Bible verses. The church was where I first learnt to stand before an audience and perform. As children we looked forward to going to church, wearing our best clothes and socialising with other children.

Mama was a disciplinarian and took sole responsibility for disciplining and training her children. She did not allow my father to hit us because she contended that he had a heavier hand, but I thought that it gave her a measure of control. She did not say 'wait until your father get home', but she applied discipline herself. She would be minded to turn a blind eye if we quickly made amends but if bad behaviour continued the discipline would be doubled. Methods of discipline included corporal punishment, since parents were in charge of children and not the other way around. Generally speaking, children's opinions were rarely sought. My parents were a product of their time and their generation. Today I disagree with using some of the methods of discipline that I received, but I understand that my parents were doing what their parents did and were following a model they were taught and observed. It was part of the cultural setting and belief system that was prevalent in their day. Parents were a product of their time, and did what appeared best to them I have always felt that communication was a far better strategy to discipline children, but be that as it may, parents held on tenaciously to their child-rearing practices and beliefs.

Lynda and two siblings.

The children Mama bore were in themselves a community and a sure way of replicating the helping tradition. Thus, our family was a microcosm of the social setting in which we were living. It was a setting where everyone knew everyone, strangers were quickly noticed and people made it their business to know what was going on. Misbehaviour was quickly reported to parents so that they could take corrective action. I recall members of the community presenting themselves at my parents' door to report to them when we acted foolishly, and it did not take much for them to complain.

Personal Reflections

Mama had many setbacks in life, but she was a strong woman with a deep conviction and a deep love for her children. It was a hard experience to lose contact with her family at the age of eighteen. This meant that she struggled on her own to raise her children. Her isolation from her two siblings was easier with the gift of her children. They became her crowning glory. As the years rolled on her strength was the one thing that carried the family through rough terrain. As I reflect on the meaning of loss, I realise that for a variety of reasons some losses may go unnoticed in the interest of finding a way to deal with the harsh realities and challenges of life. The pain might be so deep and penetrating that it is buried and remains hidden. It is a maladaptive strategy, but it keeps us functioning.

We may minimise and fail to recognise significant losses, or we may not acknowledge them, because it is too painful, or because to do so upsets the natural equilibrium and flow of life. Refusing to talk about the losses we have suffered is a reminder of our fragility and inability to hold our destiny in our hands. Yet, each loss has a significant bearing on a person's emotional wellbeing. It is only as we pause to think about how loss has affected us that we are able to focus on its impact and the strategies we have developed as coping mechanisms to mitigate the negative effects of stress.

I was coaching a lady who was struggling with looking after two foster children. As we talked about her struggles, it emerged that part of her difficulty was coping with the loss of her father. I asked her to think about the children's experience of losing their parents caused by abuse, and then separation. I asked her to consider how far she could walk in their shoes. It was this activity that led her to make an important connection since she said:

> I now realise that the loss I suffered is no different to the loss they are suffering. I am listening to you because it is getting to my heart and if you are trying to make me cry you are succeeding.
>
> (JEANETTE)

Jeanette's reflections not only became a conduit to a better understanding of the different types of losses people suffer, but moreover, to the realisation that the impact of loss is the same. It is only with hindsight that I understand the full weight of my mother's loss caused by conflict and estrangement from her siblings.

Standing at the Crossroads

> Forsake her not, and she shall preserve thee: love her and she shall keep thee. Wisdom is the principal thing; therefore, get wisdom: and with all thy getting get understanding.
>
> PROVERBS 4: 6-7 (HOLY BIBLE)

After my father passed away Mama was left with six children to care for single-handedly. Two had already left the nest. Where would her resources come from except from her inner wisdom? She stood at the crossroads with an insurmountable problem and a huge decision to make. How would she cope? And what would be her response to the sudden death of her husband and our father? The reality was that as the situation stood, she was unable to make adequate provision for her children, but in actuality, she had considerable internal resources based on her faith, wisdom gained from life experience, and a strong belief in God. The values she espoused were rooted in a statement she frequently used: 'God and one are a majority'. She did not see herself as a single parent or a victim, but as a mother with the responsibility for raising children. She used perseverance as her best strategy, not taking no for an answer. She was not too proud or ashamed to ask for help.

As we were growing up even when my dad was alive, she lived on what I would call the 'trust plan'. Her survival strategy was to ask a local shopkeeper to trust her with groceries until she could afford to pay the debt. I was often sent to the local shopkeeper to ask for supplies in return for delayed payment. In today's world, we do this but by using credit cards and accumulating debts that we cannot repay. Hence, my mother was in advance of her time, but in truth, it was a supportive community system that kept many families functioning.

In the community where I lived local shopkeepers knew families and developed a supportive relationship with them. Nevertheless, it grieved me to have to ask for groceries without the money to pay them. I would walk to the shop with my head bowed down, dragging my feet and fearful of being turned away empty-handed or being made to feel shame in the presence of other customers. Although this thought did not materialise it was a fear I carried around in my head for as long as I can remember. There are many things in life that children do not understand. One of the things I did not understand was why we had to be poor. I wanted to know why the shopkeeper took out her card and made a record of my parent's ongoing recurring debt.

Our poverty was reinforced by a system that was instituted by the government at the time to assist poor and destitute families. Kitchens were set up in a big park. It was called Queens Park. Even the name of the park was an irony because it was hardly a place for a Queen, but the site was a throwback to the colonial system. However, this was the location where food was distributed on one day of the week. There was nothing discreet about it because so many families depended on it. The hard truth was that the gap between the rich and the poor was glaringly obvious. I remember collecting the food and detested being seen walking home with it. Nevertheless, it was a means to an end. Smell and taste are two of the most powerful senses because until this day I still carry the sensation of the smell and taste of the food that was repeatedly provided without variation. It was the same every time and it carried a distinctive taste that I came to loathe.

The crossroads was a significant place to stand because it was to create the difference between poverty and survival. It called for risk-taking that took on a whole new meaning and an extraordinary level of faith. The crossroads at which Mama stood had two clear paths; the first was to remain where she was and struggle, remain in a trade that brought very little remuneration and stay on the trust plan with a dismal future for her children. The second was to take the risk of daring. The first choice would enable us to remain together, and in a place we called home. We were fortunate to own the house we occupied so it was home in every sense of the word. The second road she could take was to forge an alternative plan. Emigration was it! Plain and simple! She chose the latter.

Moving Forward

> She knew this transition was not about becoming someone better but about finally allowing herself to become who she'd always been.
>
> ANONYMOUS

It was during the first year after Daddy's death, that Mama revealed her plan to us. Transition provided the impetus and focus for a major change and a new direction. Her plan was to find a way out of this distressing conundrum. While as children we felt helpless and hopeless, she had a vision. The emigration plan had a sting in the tail because it would mean leaving five of her children behind with a stranger. Again, she had to extend her faith in order to take the leap and take what must have been a formidable step to emigrate to England to join her daughters who by this time had settled into a way of life in that far country. The broader vision was to work and earn enough funds to send for the five children she would leave behind. This was not unusual as many parents left children behind with grandparents and other extended family members – even close family friends. The point was that they conceived emigration as a way of making a new life and of forging a plan for a reunion. Economics was the factor that by and large drove these types of decisions.

Mama left the past behind and travelled to England in search of a new life. She was good at planning during times of disaster. It was as though she would go onto autopilot. To ease the separation, Mama told us that it was her intention to work and return within five years, but once in England she was distressed by the separation. This was not a unique statement for people going abroad to make, because returning to their homeland was an aspiration tied to the belief that it would be easy to find a job, and earn enough funds to return home within a short timespan. However much she searched for this dream, it did not come to fruition. In reality she met with the prospect of having to work several jobs. The path she had chosen was not smooth and her new existence was fraught with difficulties and problems she had never experienced. As a widow, she was making life on her own.

During the 1960s mass emigration was a common theme for those who were seeking new opportunities, and a new way of life. Barbados was under colonial rule, which meant that it had strong links with England, hence it was referred to as 'Little England'. Most people held onto the common myth that England was the holy grail, the ultimate. People who emigrated would, in their minds, automatically become rich and enjoy the bounties of a land that was flowing with milk, money and honey. It appeared as an incentive, and even though many leaving the island did not return, people continued to pursue the dream.

The notion of England as the mother country was one of the biggest misconceptions that many people believed, including myself. We did not know of the difficulties people faced as they tried to create a new way of life, we did not know of the culture shock or the rejection they faced. We had no notion of the racism, discrimination and prejudice they had to endure. We did not know that Mama had to revert to her trust plan in order to get the help she needed to support her application for our travel to the United Kingdom. These things I only learnt as the years rolled by and my mother unfolded the stories of her hardship and suffering.

Once in England her sole purpose was to be reunited with her children. She worked at the London Clinic and one of her claims to fame was meeting a famous singer during her work life. For the first time, she met people from other cultural groups and was exposed to other cultural values and ways of knowing; this included acculturation to the dominant cultural setting in which she was now striving to make her way and a living. During this time, she worked at more than one job in an effort to gain the funds to pay the airfare for her children to join her in this new place. I have in my possession a letter from a friend she approached for a loan and to act as a guarantor. He wrote the following:

> *Dear Mrs. Oxley,*
> *I have been thinking of what we discussed last night, and realise that for the sake of an extra £50.00 in my pocket to spend, it would be selfish not to help you when I could possibly assist someone who is making a determined effort to succeed. I have therefore decided to loan you the money and sign the papers for you.*

Further, he made reference to asking another friend to sign as a second guarantor for the airfare. Although my mother did not become materially rich, she was rich in spirit and people noticed it and were kind to her in many ways. She was contented with the little she had and taught her children the value that content with little is great gain. She taught us how to remain close and connected to each other. Her values concerning family life made us a strong dependable and interdependent family unit.

Personal Reflections

We all have aspirations of one kind or another. Generally speaking, parents want the best for their children but they do not always achieve what is best because life presents many problems and dilemmas that we often find difficult to solve. People set out with plans and high ideals but they might not work out as they intended. For many of the early emigrants from the Caribbean during the Windrush years, the dream of returning to their homeland did not come to pass because of the hurdles and barriers they had to overcome. There were no easy fixes and no quick gains. The work was hard and low paid, thus against a harsh backdrop it was impossible for many to realise their dreams, but I am glad that Mama did.

One of the valuable lessons I learnt from Mama's approach to life and problem-solving is that when we have hard decisions to make that include the lives of others, we have to be selfless in order to respond with compassion to another person's needs. The struggles we face might appear insurmountable. Nevertheless, it is only by creating a vision of what things could become that we create the possibility of winning the battle.

A difficult experience was growing up with poverty. Poverty might be thought of as a loss brought on by deprivation. It is not a loss that is physically taken away, but it can create a loss through unmet needs and circumstances. As a child I yearned for the things I did not have, I often felt ashamed, but today I realise that poverty happens to many people. We have become sophisticated at masking the truth by over-using credit cards and by creating the illusion that we have the things we do not have. We create debt, which in turn leads to stress, anxiety, fear and hopelessness. We are still trying to find ways to feed the poor by creating food banks and soup kitchens, and by giving social security benefits. In reality, whether we think about poverty at a local, national or global level, it is a problem that affects people worldwide. While it appears that we have come a long way from where I began, the revolving doors of poverty remain, but in a different guise. I can conclude that the poverty I experienced then was no different from the poverty that many people experience today.

One of the most difficult experiences in my lifetime was having to move from my country of origin not because I wanted to, but because I had no other choice. The prospect of many parents who left their children behind to find a new way of life did not always work to their benefit. Many parents lost a vital connection with their children because they were overtaken by the problems that they encountered in an unrelenting and hostile environment.

CHAPTER FOUR

Separation and Loss: Making the Transition

When Mama left Barbados, she took the third eldest of her children with her and they travelled across the Atlantic with a great deal of hope and high expectations. She went to join my two elder sisters, my eldest sister's husband and their two children. She also went in search of work. Emigration was the solution and it took her to England. The separation was painful because it came one year after the death of my father. It is separation that brings a sense of loss and sadness. During the time of separation, we suffered under the care of a woman to whom Mama had entrusted our care. This individual had no children of her own, and understood very little about how to care for children. Moreover, we did not know her. She was a stranger, but it appeared that it was Mama's only way to turn around a bad situation. This plan did not work to our advantage because the woman called Shelly was cruel beyond our imagination. My father had several brothers and three sisters, but none of them came to our aid. Looking back, it seems that while losing my mother there was either a disconnection with close relatives or they were not in a position to help. I would like to believe the latter, but there are several experiences that later ruled this out as wishful thinking. Thus, as aunts and cousins also emigrated to Canada and America, we were scattered around the world and we lost contact with them. This was another loss that represented a disconnection for me.

My memories of Shelly are not pleasant. She had returned from England and was homeless. My mother's solution was a reciprocal arrangement. This homeless woman was offered the opportunity to live in our home rent-free, in exchange for taking care of my siblings and me. This plan appeared like the golden-goose opportunity. For Shelly, it was a magical solution. It was not long before Shelly's true colours flashed like a neon sign. As my mother sent money for food, she bought it but hid it in her room and locked the door. She spent long hours on the streets selling Christian literature. She told us with a certain disdain, 'your mother didn't leave one child, not two, not three not four but five of you'. She resented the role she was playing. It came to be her undoing because she was unable to cope. Mama thought that being a woman without children gave her the time and opportunity to look after children, but it was quite the opposite. As a spinster, she lacked parenting skills and was unable to cope with five boisterous children. She also lacked love, empathy and compassion.

It was our good fortune that we had a surviving spirit. As she left the house, we catapulted our brother over the open partition and took the food we wanted, making sure to cover our tracks and conceal our actions. One of the God-given gifts we were blessed with as children was the ability to laugh heartily. We laughed amongst ourselves when she displayed her anger and hostility. We were easily amused; we were contented children and found comfort in each other's company. Having siblings was a real blessing and a life-saver.

On discovering that some of the food was either missing or had shrunk in size, Shelly was enraged. It was her rage that led her to call a man in the community who was well-known to our family, to chastise us. As we saw his van approaching our house, we took to our feet and ran in all directions and did not return home until the danger had passed. On hearing this dismal news, a church family took us in. During this time, I often stayed with my godmother. She had a husband and a young mother and baby living in her home. No one knew the father's identity, but it was believed that her husband was the father. As a child I did not understand what this really meant, thus while it was a relief to be away from the woman who had robbed us of our home, there was another danger waiting in the wings.

I was asleep the night that the man of the household, where I had visited for a sleepover, attempted to sexually abuse me. I was asleep when I felt his hand travelling up my legs. I woke startled and yelled, whereupon he quickly took flight, leaving the room not having accomplished his purpose. From that day forward, I was afraid of him, I kept out of his way and said nothing to anyone, not even my sisters. He did not bother me anymore as I didn't visit my godmother again. I often saw him in the community, but I evaded him and kept it a secret.

Abuse is one of the hardest experiences a child can go through, it is a lonely road to travel and it is one that can have long-term and devasting consequences. Many would say that I was not abused, but the fact that he touched me left me feeling awkward, and uncomfortable. I yearned to be reunited with my mother, and to feel safe again. In my work today I train foster carers about the long-term and devastating impact of child sexual abuse and how to protect and safeguard vulnerable children. I have many examples of where parents and adults refused to believe children, accusing them of lying and an over-active imagination. They fail to understand the signs and symptoms of abuse and prefer to believe that it could not have happened.

My grandmother had a nickname for me – 'Hottentot' was what she called me. It meant that I was intrepid, fearless. I believe that within my personality was the type of spirit that became my saving grace on many occasions. The incident at my godmother's home was one of those times. There were times during my childhood when I stood up to bullies and was not afraid. I knew no timidity and I fought back where I perceived that there was a danger or an injustice. It was a good trait to have, because I took it into my adult life and not only fought for myself but for those who appeared to be weaker than those who bullied them. During these times I often felt alone and as if I was carrying the weight of the world on my shoulders. I am small in stature, but big in terms of personal inner strength. This was one of the traits I gained from my mother.

Transitions involve loss and emotions that a person feels following separation. The *Oxford Dictionary* defines separation as 'the action or state of moving or being moved apart'. It is this moving apart that causes a disconnection between people who have frequent contact. It also disrupts a love relationship and strong attachment and bonds. It leaves a void. Loss is defined in much broader terms and acknowledges that a person can suffer loss for many reasons. Thus, the definition provided is 'the feeling of grief after losing someone or something of value'. Further, the *Oxford Dictionary* states that it is to do with 'not having something or having less of something'. This type of loss leads to disadvantage because something that existed is no longer available.

Loss of any kind, or at any stage of the life cycle, can be traumatic. Everyone responds to loss in different ways. During childhood, it is difficult to understand that a person will not be seen, touched or heard again. Children can begin to build up myths about themselves and about the person or part of themselves that is non-existent. The loss I experienced was because I did not know if I would ever see my mother again. But her letters and communication during this time of loss helped to keep her memory alive and thus hope burned within me.

Separation and loss bring an ending, whether it is conceived of as a positive or negative event, but it does not always bring closure because people can carry past memories, failing to let go and move forward. For example, a child who is being raised by parents where there is discord or abuse might feel a sense of relief after the abuser has passed away, as I did, but may continue to hold onto negative feelings. Nevertheless, a traumatic experience for which the child may have no coping mechanisms can signal danger. V. Fahlberg (1996) considered that adults must be honest with children in order to reduce their fear of the unknown. She states that 'even with increased abilities to understand and conceptualise, they cannot handle separation and loss without support and help'. This is the action our caregiver neglected to do for my siblings and myself during the time of separation and loss.

Transitions involve giving up basic routines, the things and activities that provide stability. When people move from one location to another it involves fear and anxiety. It is the fear that can lead to resistance and an inability to adapt and accept change. Yet, adaptation is the best strategy for growing and becoming resilient.

Throughout my professional work, I have become aware that parents and any caregiver for that matter must be able to give children security, stability and emotional warmth. These characteristics are demonstrated through a close and loving relationship that allows a meaningful attachment to develop between a caregiver and a child. From this vantage point, children are able to self-regulate their own emotions and behaviour and make easier transitions.

The new start during the early years of emigration to Britain were perilous years. It was difficult to find accommodation and black people were faced with the bleak prospect of homelessness. History speaks for itself because many of the early emigrants told personal stories of being denied accommodation and other basic life-sustaining amenities. Samuel Selvon charted the fate of the early immigrants in his book *The Lonely Londoners*. He painted a distressing picture of their struggle to find homes and work and to establish meaningful relationships. He wrote of the nostalgia of the homes they had left behind against the distressing experiences they had to endure.

Signs were boldly posted outside houses where vacancies existed. The slogan read: 'Blacks, Irish and dogs need not apply'. This meant that it was not uncommon for black families and friends to be huddled in cramped conditions with paraffin heaters for warmth. Having somewhere to live was more of a priority than was safety or comfort. There was no prospect of buying a home as immigrants were employed in low-paid jobs and banks did not lend money to black people. Those who wanted to own their homes reignited an old tradition called a 'partner scheme' because people literally partnered with each other to create economic wealth as they combined forces to save funds. As the funds accrued each person was given what was called 'a turn.' The beauty of this scheme was that the last person to cash in on their savings also got the first turn as the saving entered a new phase. Rich pickings! This was how my mother secured the funds to purchase our air tickets to join her and secure our reunion. I discovered that many families from the Caribbean were using this system because they found it difficult to get bank loans. It was how many families were able to purchase their homes and other conveniences.

My mother was in a low-paid job and the family had secured accommodation in a multiple-occupancy house. They were living in a space called the attic. It was in the late hours of the evening that the tenant below had an accident with his paraffin heater and the house went up in flames like a towering inferno. There was no escape route up or down and it looked certain that they would all perish. One of my sisters reported that her first thought was to throw out her Bible and wage packet. Today, we often laugh at her thinking but she wanted to secure her only possessions. Seen in this light it does not appear that far-fetched a thing to do, particularly as they were her most valuable possessions and as she was able to retrieve both when the commotion had died down.

Wanting to save his children from this sudden destruction, my sister's husband turned the sheets into a makeshift rope and abseiled down the outer walls of the building, but in the process broke his back. He shouted to those at the top to throw the children down, and along with the flames licking at the heels of those left behind, he attracted the attention of onlookers. People standing by summoned help, and by some strange twist of fortune they were rescued thanks to God, and my sister's husband's bravery. It was nothing short of a miracle. In the Bible there is a story in the book of Daniel (Chapter 3), about three Hebrew boys who were thrown into a fiery furnace and survived through God's intervention. This story comes to mind because God protected them in their ordeal as He surely did for my family. Another verse that has meaning for me comes from Zechariah.

> Not by might, nor by power, but by my Spirit,' saith the LORD of hosts.
>
> ZECHARIAH 4:6 (HOLY BIBLE)

They all escaped within an inch of their lives, but this sudden disaster left them homeless. After the fire, Mama, her daughters and grandchildren became homeless. It was a story that mirrored our circumstances in Barbados as my siblings and I suddenly lost the home where we had grown up. We lost the people in the community with whom we had an affinity, and although we were rescued it felt strange to be living with people who were virtually strangers. This is what my mother and siblings went through as they lived in a shelter for the homeless. They had lost everything except, that is, my sister's Bible, her wage packet and the clothes on their backs.

By way of protecting us from the horrors of what had happened, this ordeal was concealed from us until a more convenient time when the story could be narrated. Against this backdrop Mama pursued work relentlessly. One of the stories she revealed was that in her anguish and longing to be reunited with her children, she walked the streets of London and cried. These streets were certainly not paved with gold but were awash with her tears. One of the documents in my Pandora's box is a record of the attempts that were made on my mother's part to bring an end to our separation. As my mother was moving from the home where she had lived for more than fifty years, I along with my siblings who were living nearby was responsible for clearing the house and preparing her to move and live with me. In amongst her possessions, I found some records that became a significant part of my life story. These memorabilia included photographs of my parents, documents, and letters.

Personal Reflections

As people overcome setbacks and traumatic life experiences, they also become resilient. Resilience is the ability to go through adverse life events and yet bounce back. It is the spirit of survival and courage to face tragic situations without caving in, or becoming defeated. As I reflect on my mother's life, I know that she was a resilient person and the attributes she often exhibited also helped me to become resilient. Children learn to become resilient as role models provide alternative coping strategies in response to hazardous situations. Thinking back to the fire and how it changed life for my family, it has given me a sense of compassion for the homeless. Often people comment that homeless people are undeserving of monetary help. They say that they are not motivated to help themselves, that they should find work, and be more creative. I have heard it said that money given is used for ulterior motives, which can in some instances be true, but we should not judge another person's motives. I have not felt the need to judge because people end up on the streets for many reasons, some of them related to misfortune and being dealt a bad hand in life. The fact that a person is homeless does not make them less human or less deserving of help.

I can now reflect on my upbringing, and in doing so I can see that the many things that troubled me as a child have given me a new vision and a new way of perceiving the world. I can see that my siblings and I could have become homeless had not one family opened their home to us. For this I am grateful.

So, what helped me to make the long journey to becoming a successful person? I am a believer in self-development, self-improvement, self-help and determination. I do not believe that we are destined to fail or to live out a script that is created for us, but to understand the purpose that God gives us. My mother's vision involved a huge transition to the UK during midlife. Up until that time she was a housewife, but with the loss of her husband came the need to support her family. It meant that for the first time in her life, she had to work outside the home. She did not know where she was going, or where the journey would take her, but she believed that there were better opportunities. Even though transitions are incredibly difficult, standing still is even more problematic when one is looking for new avenues and new vistas.

The Reunion

It was one year after my mother's transatlantic trip when she sent good news. It was that she had gathered sufficient funds to purchase the tickets for our flights to England. Mama's greatest desire was to be reunited with her children at all costs.

Being reunited with my mother was one of the happiest days of my life. Her fortitude and hard work changed the course of my life, bringing hope and expectancy. I did not care particularly about leaving Barbados; all I cared about was being reunited with Mama. My mother was not only a woman of vision but she had great wisdom. She walked, talked and lived wisdom. She instinctively knew that disengagement or being disconnected from her children was not an option. She needed us as much as we needed her. One of the facets of her character was to walk with God and hold Him as her friend. There is a verse in the scripture from the wise Solomon that reads:

> He that walketh with wise men shall be wise:
> but a companion of fools shall be destroyed.
>
> PROVERBS 13:20 (HOLY BIBLE)

> A man who has friends must be friendly, but there is a friend
> who sticks closer than a brother.
>
> (PROVERBS 18:24 HOLY BIBLE)

The news of our reunion was met with timely jubilation, inexpressible joy and great anticipation. We were ecstatic and the euphoric feeling lasted for weeks. My siblings and I longed to see our mother and sisters again. I could think of nothing more than what this reunion would be like. It was the beginning of a transition that opened the door to a new experience. This trip would be the first opportunity to travel the long distance that did not entail the supervision of a close relative or friend. It was during this time of waiting to join my mother that I disconnected mentally with school. I remember a friend whose name was Lana. We sat together in the classroom, but when the time came to leave Barbados, I cheerfully said goodbye and did not see her again. There were other friends I left behind and they became a distant memory.

As we waited for the day to arrive, the few belongings we had were packed. I cannot recall thinking of what the weather or the people would be like when the journey was completed, where I would live, where I would go to school or how I would fit into a new culture. In my innocence, all I could think about was our reunion, the end of bad times and the beginning of good times. Reunions are about reconnecting with people we have not seen for a long time and with whom we have an attachment, an affiliation, and a bond. In my mind's eye a year felt like an eternity, within a year the waiting was ended and our family reunion became a reality.

Reunion is an integral part of the process when separation and loss occur either for a child or an adult. Reunions bring back memories of all kinds, whether good or bad. It involves looking back and looking forward. It also involves living in the present and incorporating the memories of times gone by into one's life. In trying to process my personal reunion, I understand that it was a time when I looked forward to change with expectancy but it was also a time when the reunion brought new experiences that felt uncomfortable. Learning how to deal with the vagaries of life is a skill that is learnt.

Our reunion demonstrated what is made possible when a parent is committed. I find it almost unbelievable that my mother was able to achieve the goal of bringing five children to England without the support of a husband. It seems that the focus of fighting for her children took care of the grieving. The notion of family support also came through my sisters and together they changed around the tide of circumstance, giving us choices. The rest was up to us alongside the effort to succeed. Some years later when I was training to become a social worker, I worked with a man whose mother left him behind in his country of origin. In the interim she met a man and had other children. By the time he finally joined his mother, he was not accepted by his mother's partner or his step-siblings. He found himself alone and became homeless and depressed. His poor health and his deteriorating relationship with his family eventually led to a serious mental health problem and attempts to end his life. Mama often told us that she did not remarry because we were her focus. She did not want anyone to abuse or maltreat her children.

CHAPTER FIVE

Emigration: A New Start

If there is no struggle there is no progress.

FREDERICK DOUGLASS

As my siblings and mother had done before me, along with four other siblings I was also making a transition that involved the transatlantic trip. We travelled to England during a period of British history when black people were often viewed as a threat to the British way of life. My family emigrated to England during the *Windrush* era. It was a time of great expectations and great disappointment. The perception was held that black people were stealing jobs and homes that they did not deserve because they did not fit in and did not belong. This was a view that pervaded the minds of the indigenous population. Black people were considered as criminals to be severely punished and locked away in prisons. The struggle was to integrate and assimilate into British culture, and assume an identity that was alien to them. They were denied indisputable human rights that other people were given. It was a crazy and shameful time in British history, when black immigrants from the Commonwealth struggled to settle and belong and be part of a community of people who rejected them. The Brixton riots occurred as a result of mounting tension between the police and the black community. The 'sus law', as it was called, meant that a person could be arrested on suspicion of loitering with intent to commit crime. The problem was that this practice was applied indiscriminately to black people and black men in particular. This was a time of awareness raising and a time when questions were being asked about blatant forms of injustice, discrimination and racism. It was a time when the politician Enoch Powell gave his 'Rivers of Blood' speech urging for immigrants to be repatriated. More than sixty years later we are still confronted by the same issues. It took the death of George Floyd to tell the world that *'Black Lives Matter'*. The vestiges of enslavement, colonialism, imperialism and institutional racism were alive and functioned well. It takes not only a sea change, but a heart change for people to change their attitudes and recognise that we are all God's children. The words of Floyd, *'I can't breathe'*, echoed the experiences of so many others as he was taken to his final, untimely resting place.

I was rising fourteen years old when I arrived in England and I was not prepared for anything, including the weather and discrimination. As the plane approached the runway and touched down at Heathrow Airport, it was a dismal, bitterly cold and dreary day in December 1965. The houses appeared brown and dingy; it was altogether different from the place where I had left the previous day.

My siblings and I were inappropriately clad and ill-prepared for the inclement weather. We were quickly wrapped in coats, hats and scarves and for the first time in my life I went underground and boarded a train. These were new experiences; it was a strange way of dressing and travelling. I was accustomed to running around bare foot and wearing light clothing. The place that would become my home was light years away from the place I called home. The blue sea, sandy beaches, palm trees, open doors, friendly faces had all disappeared. In exchange they were replaced with rain, snow, Kerosene heaters, bitterly cold and dismal days, with people living in huge houses with multiple occupancies.

The place where I was now to live was in stark contrast to the island I had left behind. The blue sea I knew became a sea of white faces, people who looked different from me and spoke differently from me, surrounded me. I started to hide the way I spoke; the lingo just did not match with how the people spoke in this inherited environment. When Mama gave me her homemade coconut bread in my lunch box, I hid it for fear of being asked questions. The hard truth was that I felt awkward and out of place, so I idealized the place I had come from, I forgot about the poverty and hardship in order to fit into a system that was rejecting me and stopping me from holding onto my identity. This was the first point at which I felt that my culture and identity were something to hide. In a real sense my identity was being stripped away in a similar way to how a rug is pulled from beneath one's feet.

I was forced to remember that it was not the place but the person I was longing to see. This made all the difference. All the same, the sights and sounds were alien to the ones to which I had become accustomed. I was missing my homeland and friends, the familiar sounds, and the sights I had grown up with and loved. We lived in London for a short period and then my family moved to the suburbs. It was a new town called Stevenage where even fewer black people lived, but many white families were moving out of the conurbations to find work in this rather under-developed new town.

Two of the first tasks that Mama had to accomplish soon after moving to this new town were to find a church and a job. She found both in quick succession. Mama worked at a pen-making factory called Mentmore Pens and this is where she had to contend with a charge-hand called Jim. To put it bluntly he was a bully. Each day as Mama arrived home, she talked incessantly about the degrading treatment she and other black employees had to endure throughout her working day. He frequently swore at her but she did not take it without putting up a fight. We listened as she vented her anger about Jim and the way she responded to his bullying tactics. She talked so much about him, that he almost became an invisible part of our family. This connection with her work was embedded in our family because she took the opportunity to earn a little more money by making pens at home. There was a deadline each week to return the finished product. Each member of the family had his/her part to play as we moved the different parts of the pens from one person to another. It was similar to a production line being replicated in our home. Most weekends were spent helping to make these pens. It was an industrious endeavour. A time came when my siblings and I were tired of making pens. We pleaded for it to stop but it did not end until Mama said it was over and the burden was lifted.

Years after Mama stopped making the pens, we would find the odd part around the house as a salient reminder that our home had become a factory, but more importantly, it was an *aide-mémoire* of our survival during these early days.

Everything felt strange and out of place. I had to make a quick transition and become accustomed to this new way of life. The people did not say a friendly hello, as was a habitual practice in Barbados. They simply walked on by or they stared at me with suspicion and at times with disdain or I was ignored as if I did not exist. I occupied a space where others were expressing familiarity and exchanging pleasantries but not with me. They crossed the street or preferred to stand in the bus rather than take a seat next to a black person like me. When people did have the courage to speak, they asked nonsensical questions such as, 'Did you live in a tree?', 'Do you have a tail?', 'Can the colour of your skin be washed off?'. They did not want hands to touch just in case the colour did rub off; hence, in the shops, money in small coins was dropped on the counter and I would be frequently followed around the shop and looked at suspiciously just in case I stole something.

When children looked at me intensely, parents would say to them 'Don't be rude', almost as if it was an embarrassment to be black. In fact, during those days black people were referred to as '*coloured*', as if we looked like the rainbow, had no culture, came from nowhere, and had no significance as a people. White British people were ashamed to use the word 'black' and found it offensive. I guess that the word 'coloured' had a softer tone. They wanted to touch my hair to find out something about its texture. There were references to being a monkey and children actually used that word or other degrading names that they had no doubt borrowed from their parents or family friends or

51

had picked up from the media. In fact, the media perpetuated degrading stereotypes, and some comedies were televised portraying black people in inferior positions or looking stupid. Even black people laughed and found them humorous. This lack of knowledge and understanding of the insidious nature of racism abounded everywhere.

Later on, when the local people communicated with me, they asked forthrightly, 'Why did you come here?', and... 'Why did you leave the sun to come here?'. They would jest that they longed to have a suntan just like mine. I was not aware that all of these questions were duplicitous. They did not intend to gather a true understanding of me as a person but had a deeper more insidious meaning, which was linked not only to ignorance, but also to prejudice, and racism. I felt under attack just for being the person I was. In a sense it was an attack on my identity and personhood. These truths I only understood as I began to listen to other people's experiences, as I became aware of what it meant to be a black person in a white-dominated society. I became familiar with the system, and the space I occupied which I now called home but which was far from home.

From the late 1960s onwards one of the good things that brought a positive spin into my life was the wave of music that came streaming through the airwaves from pop artists in the United States. One of the songs I remember was titled 'Young, Gifted and Black' (Bob and Marcia, song writer Nina Simone) and the lyrics of this song painted a 'precious dream' to know that 'millions of boys and girls are young, gifted and black'. Black artists were cultivating a new sense of pride by rejecting Eurocentric definitions of 'blackness' and its association with enslavement. The lyrics of popular songs brought with them the feeling of freedom, confidence and self-assuredness. Moreover, these new ideas provided another narrative more in tune with black people's lived experiences. I heard about Muhammad Ali and his resistance against oppression, we cheered him as we watched him boxing on the television proclaiming himself to be the Champion. His famous words

'I float like a butterfly and sting like a bee' were repeated in our household on countless occasions. He represented freedom of thought and speech. His fearless optimism inspired black people everywhere to think that they could dare to dream of a better life.

Wearing an Afro hairstyle made a definitive statement and communicated a message of pride in one's identity in an unspoken way. A person who made a huge impression on me during this era was, inevitably, Martin Luther King Junior; his spirit of audacity and his sophisticated way of telling the truth about the black race in the context of enslavement were a revelation to me. Alongside his motivational speeches, he planted the idea in my mind of peaceful resistance. We do not have to hate each other to fight for our rights. These ideas were liberating. His famous speech of 1963, 'I Have a Dream', motivated me to start thinking that what appeared impossible could be possible, and that any dream I had could come to fruition. His dream was that his *'four little children would one day live in a nation where they will not be judged by the colour of their skin, but by the content of their character'*. It was an ideology to which I later wanted to aspire.

Black activists like Angela Davis, Rosa Parks and Nelson Mandela were equally my heroes because they brought a new vision that there was no glass ceiling that could not be broken through, if only one persevered and overcame the struggle. Thus, it was that within my personality and coming out of the early struggles I faced, I sensed the need for justice, freedom, personhood and belonging as human rights. There became a burning desire within my soul to refute negative valuations of others based on their assumptions and notions of superiority and inferiority. I cultivated a belief system that brought abundance. As Wayne Dyer so rightly said:

> Believe that you can attain anything you wish, and that you will receive all the help you need as long as you stay focused on your goal.
>
> (WAYNE DYER 2006, P.136)

53

Personal Reflections

> Character is like a tree and reputation like a shadow. The shadow
> is what we think of it; the tree is the real thing.
>
> (ABRAHAM LINCOLN)

When we feel under-valued, it is possible to create a new narrative by cultivating a win-win spirit. First, we begin by rewriting the script that has been given to us and we write a new script that matches our reality, our experiences and our character. It is from the new script that we learn how to surround ourselves with positive people who have the capacity to help us explore our identity and our potential. I found that as I engaged with a new story of strength, my character was developed so that I was able to move along a continuum from hopelessness to hopefulness.

Although I was not familiar with ideas of self-empowerment during the early years of my relocation, I knew that people's expectations were holding me back. The notion of empowerment is when we view problems as opportunities, and we disregard other people's negative valuations in order to move forward. An important step in the process of self-empowerment is to begin by identifying one's own needs and aspirations. Self-belief is a key premise on which confidence is built, but self-doubt erodes it. Although I did not perceive the way I spoke to be a problem, learning how to communicate in this new environment was the only way that I would in time empower myself. As I reflect on this aspect of my transition during this critical period of my development, I can also see from my personal life experiences that people change who they are in order to fit in with dominant ideologies in an effort to avoid being on the margins of society.

New Environment: A Culture Shock

Experience is the best teacher; it is not only about a set curriculum, but it is also about the harsh realities of life, hard truths and making the most of a bad hand. My younger sister and I were the first two black girls in the school we attended. Denise did better than I, because she was younger and appeared to fit in with her compatriots in a way I did not. She made friends easily where I did not. Nevertheless, our introduction to the British education system came as a timely reminder that we were different from the indigenous children who had the advantages that we did not have. Another disadvantage was the timing of my immigration. At the age of fourteen I was faced with the problem of not only coming to grips with the subject matter and the different teaching styles, but I also had to cope with a huge cultural shift that threatened to engulf me. There was the pressure to assimilate into an unfamiliar and hostile environment and at the same time establish new relationships. It was a culture shock of considerable magnitude because it touched every part of my life and interactions with others.

In the school setting I stood out like a sore thumb because I did not know the fundamentals that operated in this new country, neither was I inducted into the peculiarities of this system. No one told me anything about how to make this difficult transition, but I was simply expected to become compliant. Without guidance I floundered. It was like struggling against the tide with the waves lashing up over me.

During the early days of attending my new school, I was placed in the class of a teacher I will never forget. She was called Miss Brown. She was a woman of small stature. Not only did she have a good command of the English language, but her words could be delivered with sarcasm and natural venom designed to put down and humiliate. She was intolerant and dismissive. I had the misfortune to be the butt of Miss Brown's displeasure when she asked the meaning of a simple word. I could feel her gaze and then she pointed at me to deliver the answer, but I was dumbstruck, I was fearful of making a mistake. I made several attempts to give the meaning of the word, 'record', but simply put, I could not articulate myself because I was seized with fear. Having not heard what she wanted to hear, she was frustrated and advanced her attack on me. I was humiliated in the presence of the entire class. Her actions led to support for her from my peers who reinforced her negative judgment. My sister told me that Miss Brown relegated her to becoming a shop assistant working behind the tills.

Facing racism for the first time was undisputedly a harsh blow to my system. In Barbados all I had learnt was that England was our mother country, and we were taught more about British history than our own history. The fact that I lacked confidence only served to reinforce negative ideas that came from the other side. It was the side to which I did not belong, or with which I had no affinity.

I entered the British education system at a disadvantage. My education was disrupted as a result of emigration at a critical time in my development. I came into a hostile environment and the stark reality was that I was destined to fail. Indeed, teachers did not inspire me to reach my potential simply because their expectations were low and mediocre. Like many black children, I was given poor advice and was not encouraged to see myself as anything other than a failure.

With time, other black children joined the school but in order to escape the taunting and bullying they joined forces with our assailants. One of my sisters was called names by one of the boys who had joined the group on the opposite side reinforcing the name-calling, taunting and bullying. I recall that as early as junior school my sister had her face spat upon by one of her peers. My brother jumped to her defence and was punished by teachers. As victims they were punished for retaliating and the bullies suffered no consequences. Teachers actively stood on the side-lines and allowed injustice to have free reign. As they were not part of the solution, they were part of the problem. It was a hard time growing up in the British educational system and a cultural shock of great magnitude.

I clearly recall that one day I saw a black teacher enter the school.

She was teaching domestic science. It was a subject I loved; therefore, I was very pleased to see her. She did not identify with me and I felt let down. In those days, and as a child, I did not really understand the impact that racism had on a person's identity and that many black people tried to cope with it through dissociation with people like themselves. This type of disconnection was another survival strategy. Taking this route can sometimes mean that there is resistance to acknowledging one's roots and cultural background simply to fit in with those of the dominant culture in order to make life easier. The conflict appeared to be my quest to see a reflection of myself in others, while to a greater extent they were seeking to belong. To my way of thinking they were two sides of the same coin.

People like that teacher who tried to over-conform were still equally ostracised, bullied or marginalised if they were perceived to step out of line. Simply occupying a position of authority did not grant them an undisputed place within the upper echelons of society. Surprise! Surprise! That teacher did not stay very long at my school. Unfortunately, any support I had hoped for to reinforce my identity did not materialise because it was an illusion.

In my loneliness and isolation, I looked for ways to fight back. I sought refuge and solace in the library during break periods. It was there that I met a teacher who befriended me. He allowed me to sit in the library on cold wintry days when my body temperature plummeted. I could not contend with the extreme weather conditions. He even allowed me to sit there during the summer. I am not sure if he took pity on me, or if he sensed that I was struggling. Either way, what he did made him my 'knight in shining armour'.

It was in the library that I began to read books and where I developed an appetite for knowledge. The truth is that I was hiding because I was afraid and as a result could not interact with my peers. I was afraid of being excluded, but it was in the library, in that solitary place, that I found freedom to connect with an activity that became the conduit to a better understanding of myself.

I found this reflection in a book I have read more than once. William Golding titled this book *Lord of the Flies*. He told the story of a group of British school boys who were travelling on a plane during an unrevealed period of war. The plane was shot down and the pilot was killed. The boys were left to their own devices on a beautiful desert island. The principal characters in the story were Ralph, an astute boy, and Piggy, a name he was given as an outsider. Piggy (so called) was ostracised because he wore thick glasses, suffered with asthma and was overweight. Hence, this was the reason why he was given the name of 'Piggy' and was bullied. His good advice was often ignored and the group members humiliated him because he was different. He was portrayed as the underdog and hence as inferior to the other boys, and he was treated as such. The story ends when the boys' hunting escapades lead them to become like savages, killing animals and becoming totally out of control. It was their lack of compassion that led them to eventually kill the boy called Piggy. After reading this story I recognised myself as being different and as an outsider.

Having taken my examinations, the results were unsurprisingly abysmal. When I read the results, it was akin to a self-fulfilling prophecy. The results spoke volumes after all, how could I disbelieve what was written on this important piece of paper? The results reinforced the notion that I was no good and I believed that I was no good. My first response was to replace the letter in its envelope and pretend it had not arrived. It took me several days to reveal to Mama that I had been unsuccessful.

I left school feeling a sense of abject failure. There were chiefly two reasons for this. First it was the interruption of my education at a critical stage of my development and second the lack of encouragement to perceive myself as an achiever. This course of events began under the Barbados educational system and ended with the British educational system. Children like me were told that they were not good enough and were pointed to as failures that would end up on the scrap heap of society. I have to say that this was not only my fate, but also the fate of many black children growing up during an era when expectations were very low and treatment was very harsh. I felt cheated and defeated by the system.

Personal Reflections

Education is an important part of a child's development. Without motivation, praise, stimulation and encouragement it is almost impossible for a child to excel. It is the lack of support that reduces a child's optimism and the lack of opportunity that reduces the chance of choosing a career, gaining employment to become upwardly mobile or feeling worthy to be chosen. Teachers have a duty to ensure that children are provided with the best tools to help them reach their highest potential and aspire to greatness.

The truth is that children can see themselves as failures when in fact they are not, but in actuality, the true problem lies with the lack of support and resources, which creates a disadvantage in addition to any setbacks a child might be facing. As a result of my reflections, I can see the significance of the process of transitioning from one country to another and from one educational system to another and the loss that was created by both.

During the last century educational opportunities in Britain have increased considerably, but many black children continue to under-achieve. Some of the reasons for this are the low expectations of the teachers; the lack of targeted support; peer pressure; and the failure of headteachers to take decisive action to outlaw discriminatory practices in their schools. Black children were summarily excluded from schools without being given a chance. A well-known study by Bernard Cord during 1971 exposed the plight of black children, as they were, according to him, made educationally sub-normal. Labelling and singling out children for less favourable educational opportunities was and continues to be a common practice in British schools. Much of it is also about a lack of training and understanding that diversity should be valued and celebrated in all its different forms. It is about giving every child the opportunity to succeed.

Constructed on my personal experiences in secondary school and higher education I have seen the effects of discrimination. The ability to succeed takes determination and a fighting spirit. Parents must keep abreast of their children's educational development and actively promote their success by surrounding themselves with people who are supportive and show a genuine interest in their children's progress.

Keep The Family Thriving

When all else fails, keep the family thriving. This is a lesson that families today would do well to learn and remember. In this new environment we had inherited, and away from the outside world, my mother worked tirelessly to reframe our experience. The family was the bedrock and the foundation on which we built new under-standings of the world. We were told to share whatever we had, to look after each other and to be kind in words and deeds. It was during the years of resettlement and turbulence that she used strategies to keep us hopeful. The aim was to allow us to thrive and overcome the vicissitudes of life. She could not be with us at school to defend us, therefore she used wisdom and creativity to guide her children through rough terrain. Learning how to problem-solve was at the heart of the advice she gave.

The first lesson my mother taught me was how to rely on God. On arriving in our new home her first task was to look for a church where we could worship and hold on to our spiritual beliefs. She placed a picture on the wall that boldly stated 'God is the head of this house. The unseen guest at every meal. The silent listener at every conversation'. It created an image in my mind that God's presence was with us. My mother prayed frequently and taught her children how to pray. We had the custom of going to her bedroom before we went to sleep. We were not allowed to go to sleep without thankfulness for the past day, whether it was a good or a bad day. At these times we were encouraged to read the Bible, recite texts from memory, sing and pray. Indeed, Mama often inscribed verses in the back of her Bible. One of them was taken from Romans Chapter Eleven:

> O the depth of the riches both of the wisdom and knowledge of God! How unsearchable are his judgements, and his ways past finding out!
>
> ROMANS 11:33 (HOLY BIBLE).

She formed a family choir with our voices blending. We sang together at various church gatherings. We travelled near and far to sing. At one of these occasions, we arrived at the wrong address to be greeted by a man and when we told him that we had arrived to sing he said in a typical Cockney accent (which is a way of speaking in the East End of London), 'Not 'ere you ain't'. This means in the Queen's English 'You are not meant to be here'. We turned away and laughed but underneath was an undertone of rejection. The thought he was expressing felt more like you do not belong here. It was not what he said, but it was how he said it and the message that was meant to be communicated.

Second, was that she replicated the traditions of our culture inside the home to fortify us from the outside world – she cooked soul food that made us feel good and comforted us on the inside. Her special dishes were prepared with care and love. She taught us the secret of her special dishes, which I have carried throughout my life and shared with many people. At Christmas I was selected to help her bake our famous Christmas cake. It took hours and I often complained and asked why I was chosen to do this task, but with hindsight, the secret of her delicious Christmas cake is one of the skills I have held on to with great pride. We talked, laughed around the table and shared our worries, concerns and joys. We had jolly times as well as sad times and serious times. We shared them all. Her recipes helped us to hold on to our culture and sense of worthiness. It made us feel altogether good and reminded us of our cultural heritage.

Third, my mother taught me that I was as good as any other person, and instilled in me that I should not doubt myself. When I told her of the names I was called, she taught me how to rise above it and to realise that if people knew better, they would do better. She used wisdom and wise words to fortify each of her children from within by giving them a sense of pride and self-efficacy. She gave me the impression that she was invincible.

Fourth, she taught us not to forget the past lest we should become proud and stray away from the straight and narrow path. She said that we should stay close as a family and support each other. Therefore, my family was like a microcosm of a community full of resources.

Fifth, she taught us not to be afraid and how to look to the future with confidence. My mother's way of putting across her ideas lightened the load and made life appear easier. She did not regret coming to England. She had no bitterness of spirit and she carried a cheerful countenance although life was not always kind to her. She did not have material riches, but she was rich in spirit and cultivated a disposition of gratitude.

Sixth, she told her children to choose friends wisely, to make wise choices and wise decisions. Her wisdom was both deep and wide. She never went out without a hat on her head just in case it rained, and never without a bag just in case she needed to buy food for her children. This often reminded me of when I was growing up in Barbados and she went to the market. We would constantly look out of the window to see when she had turned the corner and was walking down the avenue. She did not disappoint us, since her bag would be filled with food. She was a phenomenal woman.

Seventh, she taught us how to make sacrifices for the things we wanted to gain out of life. I observed that she did not remarry and devoted her life to keeping her children safe. Later on, as I met challenges, I replicated the example I was shown.

Eighth, her wisdom and love came from a deep place of love that each of her children knew to be unconditional. She did not marginalise or tell her children that they were incapable of achieving, but on the contrary she gave us all a sense of worthiness.

The strategies I have mentioned helped to insulate us against the outside world so that we could survive. I am reminded as I tell my story that history is replete with examples of the children of African–Caribbean origins who faced similar challenges during these turbulent years. The expectation was that families should assimilate and integrate into the system. Some parents found it difficult to care for their children and work to make a living. They were struggling to make the transition. With the inability to cope, their children were placed in the public care system, where they languished and lost their identity. The separation between parents and children was due ostensibly to economic hardship, lack of support and a misunderstanding among the indigenous population about cultural differences in parenting styles and methods of disciplining children. There was always criticism of black families and their approach to parenting.

My siblings and I were fortunate not to fall prey to the systems that consistently replicated discrimination and injustice. It was not that my mother was in an economically sound position, but rather it was her advice and wisdom that prevailed in transitioning us from childhood to adolescence to adulthood. It was her fearless nature, her ability to ask for help and her total dedication to her children that made the difference. The plans she set in place helped us to escape an abyss. We always knew that she had our best interests at heart and would do all that was within her power to make life easier for us.

Throughout my childhood and adulthood Mama had an incredible influence on my life. In discussions with my sisters, they speak with passion about her legacy. They all comment on her values and the type of person she was. Her life inspired me and helped me to overcome many travesties. Her spirit of giving and the strong attachment I made with her carried me through many difficult life experiences. In my discussion with one of my sisters her interpretation of our mother was verbalised thus:

She was a woman of true intelligence. There were times that her intelligence told her that a particular moment spoke volumes through silence. She would be sitting in the living room, with her head close to her chest, and once in a while, she would look at you when she did not realise that you were looking at her, or maybe, not. She would lift up her head and place it back down on her chest with a smile. There were times when her laugh was so large that her tummy would bubble and shake. She would crack up with laughter which made us all laugh.

Personal Reflections

In applying my personal experience during childhood, I have concluded that I had the benefit of a mother who was responsive and caring. She did not remarry but made her children her life commitment. She refused to form a relationship that could have possibly improved her financial situation but might have placed her children at risk.

I have learnt many valuable lessons and precepts from the model my mother presented as a parent, one of which was self-denial. In order to make provision for her children's needs during a critical period she grieved silently. The truth was that she hid it and we did not know the extent of her loss or her suffering. Her response enabled me to build skills that became extremely important later on in life as I faced similar situations. I had developed the coping skills to face death when I was barely out of my adolescence and preparing to become an adult.

It was the cohesion within my family, the warmth, closeness and reliance on each other that became the essence of our survival. The positive relationship I had developed with my mother and my siblings served as a protective factor. Being exposed as a child to Christian beliefs and values was also a protective factor because I was linked with and connected to a community of people and believers who provided support during an episode that could have had long-term consequences for my survival.

I took my grandson to see *The Lion King* before his eighth birthday. The well-known story portrayed a young lion called Simba whose father died as a result of the jealous, sly and cunning ways of his uncle. Simba believed that he was to be blamed because he had disobeyed his father. He found it difficult to forgive himself. As a child, he had limited strategies to deal with his grief, but with time and as he was supported and reminded of his identity it became possible for him to make the transition to another stage of development and to become strong. The love from family and friends can help to ameliorate stressful and traumatic life experiences and reduce the symptoms that are associated with loss. Strength comes through faith and the belief that we are able to overcome and grow out of tragedy. As far back as I can remember I had a secure and enduring attachment to my mother and this continued until the day she passed away.

CHAPTER SIX

Coming of Age

All we are given are possibilities to make ourselves one thing or another.

Jose Ortega Y Gasset

I left school thinking that I wanted to become a nurse but I did not have the benefit of career counselling, otherwise I would have known that it was the wrong choice. As I applied to be trained as a nurse, I was offered a place on a cadet-nursing course to eventually register for entry to the State Enrolled Nursing programme. I only wanted to become a nurse because it was the profession where two of my sisters had succeeded. It was not a dream or a goal I had set for myself. Finding one's own life purpose is critical to one's success.

Shortly after I left school and was preparing to begin cadet nursing, I had the good fortune to meet the man who later became my husband. His name was Michael. My mother was very strict and hardly ever allowed me to go out to parties and the like without being chaperoned. It was her practice to send us out in twos for protection. During the summer of 1967 a friend invited me to a party. Without discussing my intentions with Mama or my siblings, I accepted his invitation. The friend was a man who was a conductor on the local buses. He took a liking to me, but I was not interested in him so he told me that he had a friend who would be perfect for me. The thought of going alone to a party was exciting and became a constant preoccupation on my mind. I wanted to see the person he thought would be good for me. In advance of the day, I hatched a plot that would make it possible for me to attend. I planned it down to the last detail including what I would wear, how I would fix my hair, the timing of the bus to my destination and how I would introduce myself.

It was a Sunday afternoon and we had returned from church. Everyone was busy preparing the meal while I was preoccupied with getting out of the house as swiftly as I could. I managed to get away from my mother's watchful eye by telling her that I was going to visit a friend. I allowed her to believe that it was a female friend. It was a half-truth but I could see no harm in it and no other way of getting to the party.

It was a cold day and as I walked to the bus stop, I told myself that if the bus did not arrive, I would abandon the journey and return home, but as if by fate when I arrived at the bus stop the bus arrived and I was on my way to meet an unknown person on a blind date. It was a daring thing to do back in those days. But in my mind, I was reassured that I knew the person who had given the invitation, hence, I felt safe and unafraid.

The 1960's were reasonably safe times for young people on the streets. Families left their doors open; children played in the streets without fear. We did not have the gadgets that children have today and it made life less complicated, simpler and safer. Even against a backdrop of suspicion and racism, it was nevertheless a good time to grow up in the small community where I lived.

Michael was given the task of meeting me at the bus station and escorting me to the party. He arrived before I stepped off the bus; he was standing next to a small two-door car called a Ford Anglia. He was handsome, jovial, confident, tall and polite. He was older and wiser than I and he was the most caring, respectful and courteous person of the opposite gender I had ever met. At seventeen, he was to become my first boyfriend. All I knew about relationships was what I had observed from my parents and other close relatives and people in the communities where I lived. I was somewhat immature, whereas he was employed, seemed self-assured and appeared as if he had his life together. He was the complete opposite of me.

The first affinity between us was that he was a Barbadian like me and I could identify with him at this first level of relationship-building. The knowledge of originating from the same cultural group as each other gave us something to talk and reminisce about. I found out that he was a Christian and was a singer in a well-known gospel group in Barbados called the 'Cantonnets'. Apparently, the young people, mostly girls, treated this group as if they were celebrity figures. I knew of him as I often attended youth-group events, but I did not know him personally; neither did I in my wildest dreams imagine that our paths would ever cross.

Michael lived in London, thirty miles from my home. This being the case, I thought that distance might be a barrier to building a relationship with him. However, there was another hurdle to get across that needed immediate attention. It was my mother. On our first date we returned home slightly late and my mother was frantic with worry because I had left my Saturday job and did not tell her that I was going to be late. It was several hours beyond the time I should have returned home. As we approached the door she was waiting, fussing and furious. She immediately sent me upstairs and spoke privately to Michael. I did not know what took place in their exchange. After he left our door without saying goodbye, I sobbed uncontrollably on my bed and shouted, 'look what you've done, he won't come back again'. Mama's first retort to me was, 'If he cares about you, he will come back'. My worst fear was that the fox had chased away the rooster from our door, but I waited for him to make the next move. It was an anxiety-provoking time for me.

What I did not know was that in their private conversation she demanded to know about his family and his background. This was a cultural practice that parents insisted upon before they allowed their female children to get too familiar with boys. Mama discovered that she had in fact grown up with his parents and that they were respectable members of the community where she grew up. It was a remarkable coincidence. On hearing about his family, this made all the difference as she relaxed and accepted him. I saw a transformation in her attitude towards him and my indiscretion. As a result, I waited silently for Michael to make his next approach. He did so by letter, expressing regret at any distress he had caused and seeking her permission to visit me at home.

In the months that ensued he became like her son, and she loved him as if he was one of her children. One of the traits Mama possessed was that if she liked someone, she would move mountains for them. It was my good fortune that she liked Michael.

As our relationship developed, Michael wrote for a second time to my mother and made our relationship official. I felt free to see him and it seemed as though we were destined to be together. I was young and impetuous. To be truthful, I was often jealous of him because he had an endearing personality and he was well liked. My worst fear was that he would meet someone else and end our relationship because of my immaturity. As I reflected on this experience, I began to understand that it was my lack of self-confidence and self-belief that contributed to my fears. I needed him to make me feel like a whole person, so I clung to him and saw my existence in him. I had no greater aspiration than to be his wife. He was the first person who told me I had potential and that I needed to break free of the negative thoughts I often cultivated in my mind. It was a time in my life when I focused on what I could not do rather than what I could do. I was constantly putting myself down and it was a recipe for disaster. He helped me to see that I could become a person capable of more than I dared to believe.

I am truly grateful and indebted to Michael for the part he played in helping me to become a person in my own right. He presented to me the idea that there was a possibility of making something of myself. He had a moral compass that guided his life and the relationships he transacted with others. People simply enjoyed being in his company and gravitated to his warm personality. He was well known in the church he attended and was often called upon to assist and facilitate various youth programmes. His love of young people allowed him to make a valuable contribution to the work of the church and the community where he lived.

I soon discovered that Michael was a humorous person; he often had us in fits of laughter. He told jokes and his sense of humour made people want to be around him. He could easily charm the birds off the trees. He loved football and he fervently supported Manchester United. He played the guitar and piano, which gave us an open invitation to sing. He loved cricket and was an avid sports enthusiast.

Michael was a real agitator and was not afraid to stand up for what he believed in and felt was worth fighting for. I recall that one day at church he challenged the pastor as a discussion ensued about two missionaries who had gone to Africa but were asking for members to pray that they would learn to love the people. The ideas the pastor seemed to be espousing came across as supporting the couple. Mike felt that their mission was less than honourable and the discussion less than helpful, thus he openly expressed his views. He seemed to know that these missionaries had very little interest in the people but that their interest in Africa was rooted in ideological views based on inferiority. It was a discourse that was not discussed openly within our church or anywhere else for that matter. Unknown to everyone in the room this was an issue he felt passionate about, and so without fear or hesitation, he challenged the thoughts that were being expressed. There was a surprise as a sudden hush and air of silence inhabited the room.

His challenge left no doubt in my mind that he was a strong person and could express his ideas in a convincing way, no matter who he was conversing with or who his opponent might be. This was not a debate that I could enter into at the time, but I liked how he was unafraid to challenge and communicate his ideas succinctly. It was a trait I wanted to aspire to. Consequently, he became my hero and the person I looked up to for guidance and support.

As I came to the end of my cadet training, I began to send out applications to various hospitals. I attended interviews, but I faced similar problems to those I had experienced at school. I was being channelled into a branch of nursing that was less prestigious. Apparently, this was the path that most black nurses were being advised to follow. Nevertheless, I continued to visit hospitals and was offered a place to begin my studies.

It was around this time that Michael disclosed to me that he wanted to apply to the Metropolitan Police to become a police officer. He also told me that it was a career he had pursued in Barbados but did not succeed because he was rejected on the grounds that he wore glasses. He left Barbados with a brown case and arrived in England to start a new life, vowing never to return there. On his arrival, he worked for London Transport and subsequently with the Ambulance Service. He was working as a signalman for British Rail when I met him, but in his heart, it was always his desire to become a police officer and to serve his community. It was a brave and unprecedented step to take in those days, as it carried risks from the white and black community. Within the police force and the criminal justice system there was institutional racism. Therefore, joining the police force was interpreted within the black community as a sell-out. His time spent at the Hendon training centre was not without its difficulties. Blatant racism was part of his experience, but he did not allow it to thwart his intentions. Michael believed that it was wiser to create change from within than from without. When he disclosed his dream to me, I encouraged him to apply for training. He did so and became the second black police officer to be appointed to the Metropolitan Police and was stationed at Holborn Station, London. New Scotland Yard reported this as a historic event in a press release on May 18th 1970.

Michael graduates form Metropolitan Police Training School Hendon.

Marriage Proposal

We had a family custom that brought my family together for the festive season, as other families did. It was a joyous time. As we were allocated the task to dress the table on Christmas Eve, Michael knelt to his knees. He held my hand and said, 'all my love and all my life, in 1970 you'll be my wife'. He then made his proposal of marriage. I jumped for joy. I was thrilled. To the utter surprise of my family, we revealed the news. I was the second of my parents' children to be married. Michael would jokingly say, 'Mama she is the most beautiful of your daughters'. My sisters wasted no time in making their protestations.

My trajectory looked promising; I was accepted to begin my nursing career and would be making plans to begin my studies while looking forward to marriage. Michael had begun his training. However, by July 1970 I felt changes in my body and with the usual test discovered that I was pregnant. I was afraid to tell anyone, not even my mother, therefore I carried the secret for as long as I could.

One day, one of my sisters and I were in the bedroom and she asked me to lift a heavy case from a cupboard, and I bluntly refused saying: 'I can't do that'. As a nurse, she immediately suspected that I was pregnant. It was after her insistence that she knew my dilemma that I was forced to confess the need to tell my mother before my sister could spill the beans.

Mama was standing in the kitchen washing the dishes. I approached her with fear and nervousness. I gingerly told her that I was going to have a baby. She said, 'I know, but I was waiting to see when you would tell me'. Mama always seemed to know things before they came to fruition. It was as if she had premonitions. No sooner had I told her than she was thinking and planning what we would do. She expressed no surprise or anger. Her first plan was to talk to Michael. He had an older brother, who as far as my memory serves was studying law or a similar subject at Hull University. This was quite an achievement for a black person in those days, but he had received his education in Barbados at one of the elite schools.

My mother spared no time in contacting Michael's brother. She summoned him to visit us with all speed. He came without delay and was told of the dilemma we found ourselves facing. Michael's brother and my mum joined forces in telling Mike in no uncertain terms that marriage was the honourable thing to do, it was the only thing to do, and it was the wisest thing to do. Faced with this formidable task force, Michael assured them that it was his intention to marry me, but after the baby was born. This was not the answer my mother or Mike's brother was looking for, so they insisted and the date of our marriage was set for September 26th 1970. I remembered what he had said with confidence: 'In 1970 you'll be my wife'. Even if it did not happen in the way he intended, it nevertheless came to pass.

Looking back, I thank them for insisting that he should not delay his intentions. Under the circumstances, it was the best decision he could have made, because he was soon to die tragically in the line of duty as a police officer. Had he delayed the wedding I would have lost the right to any compensation or continuing financial support from the Metropolitan Police for his son.

Wedding day, Mike and Lynda.

Sudden Catastrophe

We started out our future with high expectations and high ideals. We were blissfully happy and life at this point was hopeful and full of promise. I could not see that there was anything in the world that could disrupt our happiness.

As a new recruit to the Metropolitan Police, Michael was embarking on his career. It was on the February 15th 1971 that my life was to drastically change. It was a normal day; in fact, it was an historic day, it was Decimal Day when the British currency changed. We were as happy as it was possible for any couple to be. We were anxiously awaiting the birth of our baby. It seems that in the midst of tranquillity and peacefulness, destruction was on its way; it was only that we were oblivious to it.

After spending the day together, we rested together, but a strange thing happened as he slept. For no apparent reason Michael wet the bed linen. This was completely new but it may have been that he was in such a deep sleep that he was unaware of the need to get up. I wondered if it was an unconscious fear in him that represented the tears I would soon shed. I am still unaware of its true meaning. Mike dressed for night duty and left for work.

A few hours after leaving home, he returned in a panda car, very excited because he wanted to tell me that it was the first night he would be driving in a panda car. These were the usual police vehicles in those days; they were unsophisticated and were not as safe as one would like to think. He kissed me and said, 'come to the window Lyn, and see me drive away'. We embraced, I went to the window and watched him as he drove out of the gates of the police flats where we were living at 9.30 p.m. I had no thought in my mind that it would be the last time I would ever see him, otherwise I would have done something to make him stay at home, and I would have cajoled and pleaded with him not to go to work. It was as if God wanted to give us that last opportunity to say farewell to each other. It was during the early hours of a bitterly cold morning that tragedy struck.

It was approximately 1.30 a.m. when we heard a loud and persistent rap on the door. My sister was staying with me, as our first and only child was soon to be born. It was providential that I had her support because when the sudden and expected news came, I fell apart, and Judy picked up the broken pieces.

We were startled and rubbed the sleep from our eyes, approached and stumbled to the door. Behind the glass, we could see the outline of two police officers in uniforms. We were sore afraid, so much that neither of us dared to open the door. My heart missed a beat. As we opened the door, there was terrible foreboding, I knew that something was wrong but not the magnitude of the news they brought. I looked questioningly into the officers' eyes, but before I could get the words out, one of them said, 'Mrs. Ince, there has been an accident and we have come to take you to the hospital'. I rushed to the bedroom, flung myself on the bed and sobbed loudly. My sister was also in a state of shock but she composed herself, gained control and spoke to the officers on my behalf. She quickly got word to Mama. Today I cannot remember how Mama arrived; I only know that she arrived during the early hours of the morning. In my state of distress, I summoned the courage and I got dressed not knowing what to make of this untimely news or what the outcome would be.

I can recall asking if my husband was all right and they said yes. As I understand it now, they were trying to protect me from the unavoidable news. I was in a state of panic and shock. The thoughts going through my mind as we drove to the hospital were whether he had any broken bones. What hurt had he suffered? Would he recognise me? Death did not cross my mind. All I allowed myself to think about was that he was hurting. I did not allow myself to think about death. We dressed quickly and the car whisked us off to University College Hospital, London.

When we arrived at the hospital where my husband was taken, it was how hospitals usually are at that time of night, quiet and desolate. It seemed, as I now recall, that we went upstairs and were shown into a room. Many policemen were standing by lining the corridor. I presume that these officers were his colleagues from the Holborn division where he had been placed. At the time of Michael's death, I received a card from the station, but all other contact with his colleagues ceased.

We were directed to a room where we waited for news. Minutes later a doctor walked through the door, wearing bloodstained white overalls. It was my husband's blood. I can see the doctor clearly even now. His face was the picture of death, and I knew without question that dreadful words would be uttered from his mouth. Words he could not retrieve. As he said the fatal words, I screamed and cried out from the uttermost parts of my being, 'No! ... No!' several times. No! No! But he said, 'I'm sorry Mrs. Ince, but when your husband arrived, he was dead. We did all we could, but'... and either he did not finish the sentence or I did not hear anything else that was uttered. My ears were closed to any other sounds so I could not hear him. It was in that moment, time and space that I was caught up in a whirlwind of sweltering grief and sorrow. My mind moved around in circles and I was carried away in a vortex of agony. I felt as if I had been annihilated. My pregnant body was numb and impervious to sounds. My grief was inexplicable; there were no words to explain my inexorable emotions. I was speechless, numb and dumb-founded as I came face-to-face with the harshness of death. I looked at the window in clear view, I knew that I wanted to jump and end my life but too many people surrounded me. I wanted them to go away, I wanted to be alone. The hard truth was that I wanted to die. I wanted a route of escape but there was none. I could not see how life could ever be the same again. What meaning could life have without the man I loved?

In my mind, I was young and undeserving of this misfortune; this travesty of burden was unleashed on me with a mighty force. I had seen my whole life consisting of my husband. In my thinking, he had promised to take care of us, to be our provider. We had plans to buy a home and move out of our humble police accommodation. We had plans to have four children, and now the fairy-tale story was ended. We had plans! But now it was all gone as if in a puff of smoke. It was all gone and I was left desolate. I had lost my husband when he was twenty-five years old, when he was vibrant and full of life. It was at this time that death suddenly took him without warning.

Guilty Feelings

Mike liked being in a uniform from his youth and he died in one. Against his misgivings that he might not be accepted, I encouraged him to try and he applied to the Metropolitan Police. I felt that it was my fault for helping him to get into that uniform. Therefore, I tortured myself with many recriminations and even suicidal thoughts in the hours, days, months and years following his death. I could not see how life could ever be the same without him. I had the urge to see him and asked the doctor to allow me to do so. He explained that it was not advisable, but I had to see him, so I insisted. When I saw him again, the thoughts of ending my life came flooding back into in my mind like a persecutory thought. I felt that I wanted to lie beside him and die. I kissed his forehead and he was cold and lifeless, inanimate. There was no life whatsoever, no loving response. He was gone. Then I fainted.

The next time I opened my eyes I was on the maternity ward and all I could feel was numbness in my legs where I had been injected. Whenever I opened my eyes, I continued to cry and could not be consoled. The most difficult thing for me was to believe that he was gone and would not return home. I had lost a husband, a lover, a friend, a confidant and the father of my child yet to be born. I was no longer a wife. But I became a widow. I was ushered into the ranks of singleness and lone parenthood, that is if I could make it. This was the only way I could see and express my feelings. I felt as if I had lost part of myself. The part I had gained through marriage. In the aftermath of Michael's death, I knew very little of my surroundings as I was sedated due to the level of trauma I had faced and was hospitalised until I gave birth to my baby.

My son was born nine days after the death of my husband on my birthday. It was a remarkably quick birth. It was as if God knew that my suffering was intense and He spared me the pain of a long and protracted birth. Instantaneously, I knew that my son was a gift from God, a miracle in the making. As I looked into his little face, he was undeniably a replica of his dad. I made an immediate connection with him but the dark thoughts continued to invade my mind. It is true that when an experience is painful, we want to run away and hide. This was how I felt at the time. I wanted to take the wings of a dove and fly away.

Saying Goodbye

I recall going to the funeral home to say my final goodbye to my husband, surrounded by family. As Michael lay in his coffin, I again had suicidal thoughts but the gift I was given and the network of people around me restrained me. Whatever I thought or felt did not change the fact that it was time to say my last goodbye. It was time to let him go.

Saying goodbye to Mike was one of the most difficult things I have ever had to do. I recall asking to be laid to rest with him in the grave. It was a bitter experience and one that was hard to come to terms with for many years. It was a road I had to walk alone even though I had the support of my family. It seemed that the familiar saying in the Humpty Dumpty nursery rhyme was true 'All the king's horses and all the king's men' could not put me back together again. I was totally broken and the pieces of my life were shattered like broken glass beyond recognition. How would I pick up the broken pieces and glue them back together again? More to the point, could I put them back together again?

On the day of the funeral, policemen lined the streets as the funeral procession made its way to his final resting place. People along the street doffed their caps as a mark of respect. My son sat beside me oblivious to what was taking place as we buried his father. As we stood around the grave, I sobbed and asked yet again to go into the grave with him. My son entered the world without a father, and with the prospect of losing his mother. The certain knowledge that I would be left alone to care for him, love him, give him emotional warmth, guidance, discipline and all the things that good parents do for their children weighed heavily on my shoulders. The truth of the matter was that I was gripped with fear and I felt unable to rise to this formidable task.

It was not long after Mike's funeral that another problem presented itself. I received a letter from the police asking me to vacate the premises, as they were accommodation for police officers and their families. The hard truth at this time was that I had at one and the same time lost a husband, and become homeless with all that it entailed. We were homeless and destitute. It was a storm that was wreaking havoc and mayhem at every turn. Any sense of belonging I had was gone and in its place were distress, pain and intense suffering.

I had no alternative but to return to my family home as a broken woman. It was Mama that offered me accommodation and while doing so petitioned the Council to grant me housing. She was successful, and I was given the first opportunity to rent a flat. From this humble beginning, my son and I began life on our own as I set about restructuring my life. It was during those lonely days that I attempted to record the events of Michael's death. It was no more than a few pages. I folded it and placed it in my Pandora's box. I thought no more of this note or that it would one day form the basis of a book. All I intended to do was to synchronise the events of that dreadful time.

Marriage, death, widowhood and parenthood were now inextricably linked and rolled into one big catastrophe. They all came in quick succession. These are milestones in a person's life that usually come with time and graduation. For me, the rhythm of life was lost as well as so many other stable features of my existence. The only way to get rid of the fear was to face it.

The process of grieving continued for many long years; the sobbing and crying, and pleading with God not only for His mercy but to restore my husband back to me. I experienced emptiness, nightmares, and negative thoughts as well as guilt and self-blame. Furthermore, when I learnt that two police cars had collided as they rushed to the same incident and my husband was the only one who lost his life, I was filled with rage, anger, bitterness and resentment. I asked rhetorical questions to which there were no forthcoming answers. How could life be so cruel? Why Mike and not them? How could I be so unlucky? Why did this have to happen to me? And why at this time? Why was my husband's life taken before his son was born when it was a birth he so eagerly looked forward to? Who would care for us, what would I do? I asked what the purpose behind his death was. I even constructed a conspiracy theory and clung to any idea that provided an answer or assuaged my pain. Added to my imponderable questions and confusion was the deep feeling of calamity. I began to blame myself and think that it was my fault for encouraging him to join the police force. How could I ever be vindicated? How could I ever forgive myself?

During my darkest hours of anguish, I turned to God and I prayed that the strong and incessant feelings for my soulmate would subside. I did not know how this would happen but I kept praying and looking for an answer to my prayers. A verse in the Bible I often turned to told me that:

> The eternal God is thy refuge, and underneath are the everlasting arms: and he shall thrust out the enemy from before thee; and shall say, Destroy them.
>
> (DEUTERONOMY 33:27 – KJV).

This verse gave me comfort and hope because it made me feel as if there was a power outside of myself holding and lifting me up. It made me feel that there was a place I could run to, a refuge I could flee to, and it gave me hope through an extremely perilous time of bereavement and loss. God had promised that my enemy, namely death, would be destroyed.

Personal Reflections

There is a purpose behind everything that happens to us, and although we do not always see or understand why we go through difficult experiences, it is true that even in the bad times some good can come out of them. The death of Michael was the hardest truth I have ever had to face. As I look back at the various compartments in my Pandora's box, I am able to retrace my steps. The birth of my son was mingled with trauma, grief and sadness, yet he was the best thing that could have happened to me at that time. I saw that death and life were inextricably linked. I can look back with hindsight and think of the purpose for meeting Michael when I did and the joy it was later to bring even without him by my side.

Trauma comes to a person or a community of people as a result of a tragic incident. It is only those who survive who are able to tell the story, and in so doing help others, but they are only able to help others as they are healed and become empowered. Even if we walk in a person's moccasins for a mile, we will not truly understand it because it is the gravity and weight of the loss that are mystifying to most people. It is difficult to define human feelings and emotions because they are different for everyone, but Karen Onderko defines trauma as:

A deeply distressing or disturbing event that overwhelms an individual's ability to cope, causes feelings of helplessness, and diminishes their sense of self and their ability to feel the full range of emotions and experiences.

Bereavement at any time in the lifespan can be traumatic depending on the circumstances in which it happens. If it is expected, we have time to prepare, but when it is sudden and is linked to another possible traumatic event such as giving birth, the trauma is intensified and magnified. To undergo sudden death at the same time as giving birth is a huge burden to bear. Trauma leading to grief becomes complicated when we find it hard to accept experiences that are emotionally crippling. I have no way of explaining how I survived that most perilous day, but with reflection I can only say that my survival was strongly linked to an unshakeable belief in God's mercy and His care for me.

There is a difference between what Kubler-Ross and Kessler (2005) call anticipatory and sudden grief. The sudden loss of my father, which I spoke about earlier, came again to me for a second time and within a relatively short space of time. It was just eight years between the two losses. This time it came in the form of a shadow at my front door. I was a newly married woman. I was pregnant with my first and only child. Truth can be cruel when it is unexpected, unwanted, undeserved and unwarranted. It is hard to accept death when it is sudden and there is no reason for it and there are no justifiable answers. Nevertheless, my biggest question was simply 'why?'.

Anticipatory death gives time for the grieving process to begin. It can soften the blow. Knowing that death is coming also allows the dying and others to make amends, to reflect on their life and to make spiritual and practical preparation. From a Christian perspective there is time to ask for forgiveness, to make restitution and prepare for the inevitable. My story holds both types of grief.

When I reflect on the experience of losing my dad and losing my husband, I have concluded that while they were both sudden and traumatic, I was more severely affected by the loss of my husband because of the connection we had, the level of my dependence on him, the harmony we enjoyed, and attachment that was part of the husband-wife relationship. Getting through this level of loss could only come with time and acceptance. I only have one answer for my survival. It was my spiritual beliefs, and certain knowledge that God would carry me through my sea of despair and anguish. I hoped that He would bring me out at the other side of my fears. It was my trust in God that gave me the will to live. These are the factors that contributed to my healing and eventual recovery.

Coming of age is usually associated with excitement, transition, moving on, with hopefulness and expectancy. My coming of age was undergirded with the opposite of these things, and in their place were grief, loss, disappointment and unfulfilled dreams. I could only recover by taking one day at a time. In the immediate time my only option was to jettison my dreams and focus on my son and my own survival. I did not return to a career in nursing. I spent time at home jointly caring for my son with my mother.

There are several examples of loss in the Bible that gave me hope. The story of Naomi is found in the book of Ruth chapter 1 (HOLY

BIBLE). We are told that during a famine she, her husband and sons were forced to emigrate to another country. After some time, Naomi's husband died and she was left to raise her two sons as a single parent. Her sons intermarried with the women of another cultural group. Disaster struck again when both sons died. With the loss of her entire family, she was forced to return to her country of origin, where she was rejected. She wanted to change her name to 'Mara', which meant that she had gone through a bitter experience. Naomi's faith, her belief, and her trust in God became evident as she fought back against the devastating effects of the loss she had suffered.

For me, trusting God was a key factor in my survival because I did not know where to turn to for help. There were several Bible verses that gave me hope and encouraged me to hold on and wait for a better day. I had to believe in God's providence and His grace because I could not do it for myself. I had to believe that He would not allow me to go through more than I could bear. That notwithstanding, the emotional pain was real and it continued without diminution.

Day after day, I cried and asked God to help me bear the pain. It was an emotional struggle and very difficult to contain because my world was turned upside-down. I felt as if a part of my soul and my inner being had been stripped away. Nevertheless, I learnt that His grace was sufficient. As I surrendered and went through the valley of this traumatic experience, I learnt how to be courageous. I learnt how to get through the bitterness, the pain, the fear, the agony and the disappointment. It was in doing so and with the passage of time and with patience and perseverance that I learnt the art of acceptance and with it my recovery eventually came.

Based on my personal experience I know that death is considered to be one of the highest predictors of harmful and devastating stressors that anyone could go through. It is the Hard Truth. This is because it carries high risk factors that can lead to a chain of unwanted events. It took me through a rollercoaster of emotions and a cycle of despair.

Having the internal resources to cope with the range of emotions that came in its wake was a key factor in my survival. The question is how I was able to break free of the risk chains and avoid getting trapped. It is now that I can reflect on the prime reasons for my survival.

The first was to develop strong faith and belief in God's benevolence. In my favour was the fact that I had been raised in an environment where I was taught how to pray. I was taught how to rely on God. It was my belief that God would reconcile and make my life better, by giving me inner strength. He did it in advance of the event by giving me a gift on which I could focus and gain comfort. The gift I was given ultimately became my way of escape.

The second step was to develop hopefulness. Although hope can seem like an illusion when a person is going through the finality of death, it is the best way to overcome the shock and bewilderment that accompany death. Hence, I held onto what the Psalmist David said when he met many struggles and was fighting for his life. This beautiful psalm gives comfort, hope and reassurance, since it takes every negative aspect of life and turns it around into a positive. Thus, it is stated:

The Lord is my shepherd;
I shall not want.
He makes me to lie down in green pastures;
He leads me beside the still waters.
He restores my soul;
He leads me in the paths of righteousness
For His name's sake.
Yea, though I walk through the valley of the shadow of death,
I will fear no evil;
For You are with me;
Your rod and Your staff, they comfort me.

PSALM 23: 1-4 (THE HOLY BIBLE)

Accepting My Gift

My son was born on February 24th 1971. It was on my birthday and he came to me like the refreshing rain. He was the best gift I had ever received. Amid the grief I was celebrating the beautiful gift of life. I did not know until then that God gave such generous birthday gifts. I received an unusual and fitting gift at the right time and in the right place. His appearance into the world helped to dispel the foreboding fear, even though the battle ahead would be a long and arduous one. As I held him in my arms, I knew for sure that he was a gift from God. I knew he was not his father – although he looked like him, he was not him. The other twist in my story was that when I was pregnant one of Michael's brothers who was living in Barbados died of leukaemia. He had written a distressing letter to me expressing his grief for the loss of his brother. He was distraught and asked me if we could give our child the same name as his brother. He believed that his child would be a boy. He wrote a sad and compelling letter that was foreshadowing what I was to feel only a few months later. The letter was dated 6th September 1968 and he head it: 'At Work'.

> *I am still feeling the effects of my brother's death, as a matter of fact, I feel it more now than the day I received the news. I could not believe it. On consolation, he was a Christian. I need your company now more than ever. Nevertheless, I probably am better off in solitude than with company.*

When I saw my son I felt sure that he should not be given his uncle's name. There was a reason for even the way my son looked and how he was born. My senses told me that he was an important little person. I do not believe in reincarnation, but this was a strange phenomenon because he had a strong resemblance to his father that was glaringly obvious. I gave him the exact name of his father – Michael Eaton DeLisle Ince. Over the years I have watched him grow; his mannerisms and his attitude to life are exactly the same as those of his father. How could he be the same as a person he had never met? I believe that it was a miracle and not something that could be explained in human terms. There has to be something that is inbred, that is created, fashioned and formed by the hands of God, and God alone.

On receiving the gift of a son, I was glad I did not leap out of that window because I could see the makings of something beautiful. I developed an attitude that it was my son and I against the world. I exchanged the notion of ashes for beauty. I was determined to make a life for us whatever sacrifices it would take. This way of thinking was the greatest motivational factor on the road to my recovery.

Family And Supportive Relationships

The family is surely an enduring legacy and when God gave me a big family and a mother with a heart of gold, He knew exactly what He was doing. My family surrounded me with love and a special type of care. Each member acknowledged and played their role. Family gatherings, praying together and having fun were a particularly important aspect of the strategies that worked well for me through a traumatic period. As a family we had a practice of having lunch together on Sundays. As we sat around the table Mama would always find a reason to bring Mike into our conversations. At these times I listened but did not respond. Her strategy was a wise one, because it kept his memory alive and even if I did not communicate my feelings, I was allowed to remember him.

I felt the love and support of each member of my family. As they gathered around, they physically and symbolically embraced me. Their support was unconditional and guaranteed. It was an emotional time for all of us. They consistently supported us in various ways for many years – ways that are too numerous to mention. The importance of family as a protective structure against the vicissitudes of life was a legacy that my mother in her wisdom had created. It was the truth about family cohesion that was a big part of my saving grace.

Friends were also an important source of support. When I eventually opened my Pandora's box, I saw the cards from people I had long since lost a connection with but who were there at the time. I revisited their words and sentiments. My senses told me that they came into my life at a specific time for a specific reason.

In my experience, the best form of support came from family members since it was a time when there were few community resources available to call on. Without access to counselling or therapy I was forced to rely on my family for different types of support. Whether or not professionals were aware of it, very little was done to help those facing the trauma I was experiencing. Therefore, when I asked for help it was not forthcoming. Indeed, I was dismissed empty-handed and with a few meaningless words. I felt let down by the system.

The concept of family means different things to different people and is culturally defined. One of the organising principles of black family is oneness and harmony. 'I am because we are, and because we are, I am.' (Mbiti 1970:141). The extended family is made up of and defined by its interconnected kinship networks (Ince 2009:74). I had a large extended family but emigration separated the family so that some remained in Barbados, some emigrated to Canada and others went to the United States. This meant that in terms of practical family support the only members I could rely on were those who were immediately within my family circle. They were living in close proximity and were available.

When the family unit works well and utilises its strength it can become a reservoir for survival even if it is against the odds. Mama taught us that the family which prays together stays together and I have proved it to be true. During my time of bereavement, my mother looked after my son for the better part of the first two years of his life. One sister, Pauline, who was recently married at the time, allowed me to live with her for a short time, and other siblings helped in practical ways.

Lynda and Michael.

My brother, Daryl, became a significant figure in my son's life and a surrogate male role model for him. I have spoken to my son about the roles his grandmother and his uncle played in his life and he stated:

> *If it wasn't for you and Nana I wouldn't be where I am today. I've been lucky, things have worked out well for me, and I'm in a relatively good position today. Much of it came from you along with perseverance, keeping my head down. Yes, I was bright, but I also had to work hard and some luck did come into it.'*

Further, he said:

> *I didn't miss out because it was like I had two mothers. You were my mum and my dad and Nana was also my mum. She made me feel special so I didn't feel as if I missed out on anything.*

Of his uncle he said:

> *I would get intense excitement whenever I knew I was going to see him.*
> *I looked up to and aspired to him. I put him on a pedestal, he was an*
> *amazing person.*

From the earliest days, I was able to take Mike to the United States to visit Aunty Gozil, and his paternal grandparents who were at the time alive and living in Barbados. These experiences exposed him to travel and gave him insight into different ways of life and diversity. It helped him to connect with family members who did not live close by but with whom I had a close relationship.

As a parent, I made decisions that were in my son's best interests, widening his horizons by allowing him to see the world through different lenses. I instinctively knew that our lives could change if only we persevered and got through the difficult years.

I did not have any special knowledge of child development through Mike's early developmental years but I knew in my heart of hearts that I should put his needs above my own. What helped was the way we established an attachment that bonded our parent-child relationship. We were attuned as we shared good and bad experiences together. He knew that I was always there for him. He was given a stable home and a positive, caring and loving environment in which to develop.

Bowlby (1973) and Winnicott (1988) carried out research on attachment and declared that it is essential for young children to establish a secure attachment with a primary figure during the early stages of their development. From an African and African-Caribbean perspective the wider family and community have a significant role to play in raising children. In particular grandmothers are considered to be critical in supporting parents and bonding with their grandchildren (Ince 2001). I believe that it was my early attachment with my parents and wider family members that was a critical factor in how I was able to support a positive attachment and relationship with my son. It would have been easy to focus on my pain and exclude him, but I made a conscious decision that to do so was not a path I wanted to follow.

I have found the process of reflection to be an integral element of my personal learning and development. It has taken me over forty years to be able to write my reflective thoughts surrounding the death of my husband and the birth of my son and to share them publicly. Although it has been a difficult task, it has also been cathartic. Loss of a love relationship was one of the things I cried about for many years. As I reflect, I can see the journey and the path that life has taken me along. I felt as if I was caught up in a whirlwind and was carried along by circumstances.

When an adult loses a partner the physical aspects of the relationship disappear, leaving a void that is difficult to fill. Jane Littlewood (2014) identifies these losses in specific terms. For example, she states that there is 'loss of a confidante, a sexual partner, social role, economic deprivation and alternative childcare arrangements.' While my family provided alternative childcare over a long period, all the other factors she mentions were present.

In terms of my personal awareness and the ability to reflect, I have used journals as a way of expressing my thoughts, emotions and feelings. The reflective process begins by describing one's feelings and ends with actions that promote problem solving. Journaling was one of the actions I took that became integral to the healing process alongside family support, reliance on God and a strong foundation of faith. These methods gave me agency in working through feelings of despair, helplessness and hopelessness. As I look back it is possible to see how I made it out of a dark place. The defining moment for me came out of a crisis and it was unfortunately the very time when I had to face the hard truth. It was the time when I had to grow out of my truth, and one of the hardest choices I had to make was to accept it. Kubler-Ross (2005) pointed to five key stages that are commonly associated with grief. In reflecting I recognise how my emotions were affected.

Stage 1: Denial

It took me many years to creep out of denial. I was overwhelmed with grief, but it was only as I reflected years later that I could see the levels of grief and trauma I had faced. I felt as if the rug had been pulled out from under my feet and there was nowhere to stand as a chasm threatened to engulf me. Life had dealt me a terrible blow.

Stage 2: Anger

During the ensuing and dismal months and years I felt that what had happened to me was unfair. The questions in my mind were: How could this be? What had I done to deserve this? I had withdrawn and shielded myself from questions, and from pity. The question in my mind was always 'Why me?'. I was angry with everyone including God, but I felt the most anger I harboured was against those I felt had caused my husband's death and against those who had escaped with their lives intact. It was also during this time that I began to ask the question: How could Mike leave us to fend for ourselves?

I believe that the manifestation of my anger was to apportion blame.

Stage 3: Bargaining

The third stage of the grieving process was tortuous because I wanted to reconstruct my world. I began talking to God and I said 'if you do not let this happen to me again this is what I will do'. I bargained with God that if He did not allow anything to happen to my son, I would become a good mum to him. I bargained with God about many things. As my son moved towards his 25th birthday I was terrified that I would lose him as I had lost his father. Thus, I continued to bargain.

Stage 4: Depression

Feeling depressed is a normal stage that follows grief, but what I did not know was that it could become complicated and complex unless I was able to respond positively to negative feelings. Isolation and forcing feelings inside were a major cause for drifting into depression.

It was not far from my door. This is why the support of my family was a key factor in my recovery and even though I wanted to keep my feelings hidden I was often reminded that my husband was a good man who wanted the best for us. It was not his desire to die; it was just a set of circumstances that worked against him on that fateful night and I was trapped in its vortex. The fact that we cannot see into the future is primarily the reason that we cannot stop impending doom. The only solution is to learn how to cope with the aftermath of death, deep loss and grief.

Stage 5: Acceptance

Acceptance was the stage when I began to turn this tragedy around – it is the ability to put closure to an event while not forgetting. It was when I began to turn my mind to avenues that could be explored, as I concentrated on working towards my survival, that change slowly came. It was during this stage that I began to see options and possibilities. The keyboard that Michael left behind provided a new focus and an aim. I focused on the future and it provided a way of escape. In her book, *Faith in the Valley,* Iyanla Vanzant makes a valid point when she states that 'confusing, tragic, painful events will come and go. These events cause shifts in our minds and upheavals in our hearts for which we need time to grieve, heal, understand and accept.'

Personal Reflections: Turning Grief Around

In my experience acceptance is not the final stage of grieving. There is another stage that I have identified as Turning Grief Around. During this stage, a bereaved person can begin to develop tools that bring healing by reversing the way they are thinking. The way to turn grief around is to go back and revisit established coping methods. I looked at how I had coped in similar situations where I had experienced similar losses. I found that the death of my father, the loss associated with moving away from my country of origin, migration and my early experience as a migrant all helped me to turn my life around. These experiences were not in vain, but they consolidated my understanding and internal coping mechanisms. During the turnaround phase, the focus is removed from disappointment to greater fulfilment. It is during this stage that faith is the key element driving the narrative of success. What might have appeared as immutable defeat is turned around as steps are taken one by one to build a new future.

Ten Self-Help Tips For Turning Grief Around

- Do not hide from or deny the challenges you are facing, but confront your fears.
- Recall and practise past coping mechanisms that worked for you.
- Develop a spiritual response to grieving by working in partnership with a source that is greater than yourself.
- Remain connected to people who are able to give support.
- Seek professional help such as talking therapy.
- Take a problem-solving approach.
- Take one day at a time.
- Build confidence in your ability to cope.
- Learn from defeat.
- Focus on success rather than setback.

The above tools I am offering come from insight and self-awareness and are based on many years of struggling to grow out of grief.

Becoming a Parent

It is claimed that there are no books that can teach a person how to parent, and to some extent, this is true. However, we often forget the teacher who is more often than not the true model. Parenting is a challenge if parents are unable to love, nurture, and provide a stable, secure and safe environment for children. We learn to parent by absorbing the examples we see and grow up with. I have seen this during my career and working with children who have been abused and neglected by their parents, and unfortunately by subsequent caregivers.

Becoming a single parent was tough but it also had a positive spin for me because I could devote my time and efforts to parenting my son. It made me a stronger person and it gave me some valuable tools to use. Some of the tools were sharper than others, but they were all utilised with the intention of learning from my experiences and became a stepping stone to helping others. It seems that I was destined to follow in my mother's footsteps, but for what reason I did not know or understand. At this stage of my life, duty and responsibility were the biggest driver in the actions I took. It was up to me to pass on to my son the values I was taught throughout my life. My strongest duty was to provide a safe, caring and stable environment. My strongest responsibility was to love, protect and provide for my son's needs. I had the desire to accept my duty and responsibility which meant that half of the battle was won.

By the time my son reached the age of three, I recognised that he was a gifted child. My husband had left behind a small keyboard and Mike would sit at it attempting to play. I immediately sensed that he could be a talented child. I wasted no time in taking him to the local music school and registered him for piano lessons.

I recall that his music teacher was a flamboyant woman. On the day we first met her, she breezed into the room wearing a distinctive pink cape, and high-heeled shoes. She had long flowing hair and looked like the very picture of exquisiteness. She immediately developed a liking for Mike and they got on like a house on fire. Where other parents brought their children and drove away, I stayed and sat in on his lessons. It was in so doing that I developed a positive relationship with Cathy. In this way, I followed his progress avidly and took notes of his homework. I invested in a piano and ensured that he practised for at least half an hour every day after school. Having accomplished this

task he was allowed to spend time playing with his friends or engaging in other activities that he enjoyed such as visiting the library to choose his favourite books, or playing games – one of which was Scrabble. This is a game we enjoy playing together to the present day.

Music brought joyfulness and dynamism to our home. It was not long before our home was filled with the music of the great composers. Mike loved Chopin's music and would play it incessantly. I entered him for competitions at the local Gordon Craig Theatre Talent Show. He won the trophy for these local competitions for three successive years. His 'hat trick' was reported in the local *Gazette* newspapers. As Mike received his trophy it was stated that he was so little that his feet could not reach the pedals. The audience gave rapturous applause.

Mike successfully completed each music examination and by the time he was eighteen years old he passed the final Grade 8 with distinction. His pass mark was 140 out of a possible 150. This is the examination he speaks about as one of his greatest achievements. He said, 'when I was finished playing the examiner said I enjoyed that' to which he replied 'So did I'. He has quite a sense of humour, similar to his dad.

At school his teachers saw the same talent and he became a member of the school orchestra and played at assemblies, parents' evenings and school functions. He was a delight and the envy of many parents. Everyone knew that he was destined to make something of his life. He was the church musician from age nine years until eighteen when he left home for his university studies. As we were a singing family, he was often our accompanying pianist. I felt extra proud to be his mother.

It was when we went on holiday that I noticed a musical event that I thought would be of interest to him. The Bournemouth Symphony Orchestra was playing Tchaikovsky's Violin Concerto. The sheer enjoyment of this concert led to a yearly celebration between us that has lasted to the present day. It was and still is the Proms at the Royal Albert Hall and any musical festival that catches our imagination.

Focusing on giving Mike opportunities to excel was a good strategy because he responded well to my methods. We worked like a dream team, harnessing our energies and personal resources. As a parent, I organised activities for him to do, including setting off in the car to visit museums and places of interest. He was an avid reader and by the age of seven, he had a reading age of a ten-year-old. We spent time visiting the library where he could listen to stories and choose his favourite books. He had an intense interest in dinosaurs, knew every possible species and knew their difficult pronunciations. He was like a walking dictionary. When it came to bedtime and lights out, I discovered that he hid a torch under the sheets and would read long past his time to sleep. He was good at debating and had special reasoning and cognitive abilities. He would make pronouncements that would make people laugh. Against the tragedy and being born into a harsh environment my son was the gift and the blessing I received that made the difference.

One of the activities that children enjoy is going on holidays. Taking holidays was an important event in my calendar so we travelled together so that he was able to experience life in different places, particularly the United States. Although fearful, I allowed him to visit my sisters for the summer. It was an exercise that gave him freedom. It seemed as if everywhere we went there were kind people who showered us with love.

Personal Reflections

Many people think that children need two parents and while this is the ideal there are children growing up in single-parent families that survive and make it to the other side. What is required above all else is for children to feel unconditionally loved, wanted and secure, to be given stability and to enjoy a consistent pattern of parenting where there are routine and boundaries. Discipline and providing the tools that will help children become resilient are a key function of parenting. If single parents can develop these qualities, they will be able to help their children develop normally and enjoy life. It was after the death of an African child at the hands of her aunt that the Government at the time published a document called 'Every Child Matters' (Crown Copyright). It mattered that every child should be kept safe, and given opportunities to enjoy and achieve. There was an expectation that parents and guardians should make provision for children's economic wellbeing and as they mature help them to make a positive contribution to society. As a young parent, I did not automatically know these things, neither did I put them in this sequential order or framework. Nevertheless, I parented from my heart and from the model I was given. It was also from my natural instincts that I did these things.

The goal of parenting is always the same whether a child is raised by a single parent, two parents or within the extended family network known as *Kinship care*. Even though in my son's case he did not have the opportunity to meet his father, he benefited greatly from my extended family and the interest that my brother took in him. My brother had the compassion and the strength of character to be a role model and he filled the gaps through his male influence. Thus, the support my brother offered was of critical importance to Mike's survival because it influenced his life in numerous ways. The most influential thing he did was to teach my son about manhood, about courage and how to become responsible. He instinctively knew that this was important because like my son, he grew up without a father. Thus, he felt the pain because he knew the pain. He did not fail to follow Mike's education and show an interest in his development. As a sports enthusiast and football lover, he engaged Mike in sports to strengthen his character. These were the building blocks he put in place to support my son's development.

I can say with strength of conviction that single parents are capable of supporting their children to become successful – that is, with the caveat that they are willing to make personal sacrifices. It is essential for parents to recognise the need to enlist the support of others, so that their children can benefit from a balanced and broad-based approach to parenting. I have delivered training programmes to teach practitioners how to develop a sound knowledge of how to work positively with parents and help them develop parenting skills. I was often surprised at the lack of awareness and empathy that many practitioners had towards single parents.

Today, I observe how my son is fathering his son. I am encouraged by the love and patience he demonstrates. I am impressed by the way he provides opportunities for my grandson (Lenny) to become involved in activities. His parents noticed that he had a gift for swimming and they encouraged it but also allowed him to enjoy this activity without undue pressure. This has helped him to develop routine as he attends his lessons. Furthermore, I have noticed that this has caused him to become committed to a personal and positive endeavour. By the age of eight, he had won several certificates, medals and a trophy for being the best swimmer within his age category. Parents must create a vision in their minds of how to help children reach their full potential.

*Lenny wins two gold medals for
swimming.*

*Lenny wins trophy swimming
championships best boy aged 8.*

CHAPTER SEVEN

Fighting Back

A journey of a thousand miles begins with a single step.

(CHINESE PROVERB, LAO TZU)

I was on a journey. I had no conception of its final destination, but I knew that if I wanted to control my journey, I would need to keep moving. There is no planning that can truly prepare a person for the aftermath of death; it is a process that we have to go through and negotiate. It helps if we can begin to take small steps to carry us towards the end of the journey, which is when we come to a station called healing. Healing came as I turned around my misfortune, growing steadily out of adversity to become resilient.

The only way to grow out of adversity is to fight back. It was learning that out of my suffering came unusual and extraordinary gifts and equivalent good. It was only that I did not know it, or how I would eventually move far beyond the point of suffering. I do not know where I got the strength from to fight, but it came. As human beings we have a wonderful inbuilt defence system within our DNA that springs into action even though we may not be consciously aware of our behaviour and actions. We can fight situations head-on as we face them, we can take flight by choosing the road of least resistance, we can freeze emotionally making it impossible to express emotions or we can submit and become victims of our circumstances. I chose the first option as I was forced into a position where the need arose to engage in a battle for compensation for the death of my husband. It was the only way I knew to create the financial means to provide for my son, thus the other alternatives were not viable options or escape routes I could take.

The decision to fight for compensation was a brave step to take at a time when I was grieving. It began with the realisation that I needed to be financially independent and stable. If I were going to dig myself out of the trenches, I would need to become proactive in planning a way to outlast the tragedy that had befallen me. I instructed my solicitor for the Police Federation to act on my behalf. The intention was to make an application for compensation from the Criminal Injuries Compensation Board so that justice could be done. This was because my husband died in a collision with another police vehicle as he was responding to an emergency 999 call. It was believed that terrorists were attempting to gain entry to a barracks at a Territorial Army Headquarters and he had been called to respond in an emergency. When I was told of the extent of his injuries, I felt the will to fight for justice against a system that threatened to leave us destitute, homeless and penniless.

When my case was heard it was decided that I was not entitled to compensation because my husband had taken a risk. I refused to take no for an answer and thus instructed my solicitor to make an appeal to the High Court. The battle to win compensation took two and a half years. It was on July 21st 1973 that three judges backed my appeal and ruled in my favour. Their judgment was reported in the national and local newspapers under the heading 'PC's Widow Wins Long Fight for Compensation'. (North Herts Gazette Series July 26, 1973). Lord Denning, Master of the Rolls, said:

PC Ince took a calculated risk in the cause of his duty. It would not be right to expect a policeman in the course of his duty to take reasonable care for his own safety.

Lords Justice McGaw and Lord Justice Scarman agreed with his ruling.

The next day, the media unexpectedly arrived at my mother's home where we were visiting and I was interviewed. During this interview a comment I made was: 'At last justice has been done', because I truly believed that the first ruling was unjust.

It was as a result of fighting back that I won my case. This was my first victory and vindication. The headlines read 'Award for PC's Wife', but it was not until I read this article that I realised that the emergency call that Michael responded to was a false alarm. Effectively, my husband's death came about as a result of false information. Another victory was that due to the success of my appeal, the Police Federation said many cases could be reviewed in the light of this decision and asked the Home Secretary to direct the opening of past cases. They said:

> *This is a great success for the federation. Up until now we have been faced with the situation where a policeman might be penalised for taking a risk in the course of his duty.*

Thus, in fighting back, I not only helped myself, but many others who had been turned down benefited from the justified position I had taken. As it was a test case the outcome was cited in the law books. In a strange way good came out of a bad situation. I had not only won my case, but I had made history as others would now benefit from my suffering and my actions. It was the desire to fight at a time when I was weak that brought strength.

When I finally received compensation, it was two and half years after Michael's death and we were living in rented accommodation. My financial resources were limited because I was out of the workforce and was living on a small police widow's pension and a grant for little Mike. This was because my husband had only served in the Metropolitan Police Force for a few months.

I decided that I would purchase a home where Mike and I could settle. At the time I was attending an Evangelical church and the pastor and his wife were very genuine people. They knew that I was looking for a home and said to me that they were moving from a spacious four-bedroom property and gave me first refusal to purchase it. I made it a custom not to make any major decisions without consulting Mama; she was my friend and constant guide. At this time of searching, we prayed for a sign from

God. We wanted to know that this was where God wanted us to settle. When we viewed the property, I thought it was too big, but Mama said, 'Lynda, it is the home for you.' I was afraid of the weight of responsibility I would carry with looking after such a big house alone. I said to her, 'But Mama, it is too big'. But she said: 'Lynda, if you would listen to me, you would make a wise decision.' While in doubt, consequently I listened to her because I trusted her. I bought the house and it turned out to be a wise decision. I was kept close to my family and I had support that buffered and pulled me through a difficult time in my life. I lived next door to extremely caring and helpful neighbours.

Several years had passed by and I heard nothing from the Metropolitan Police, although we were not totally forgotten. I had intermittent contact with the Welfare Officer and I was able to write and ask for financial support when it was needed to help pay for Mike's education over a period of seven years, enabling him to complete his medical studies. They supported him well beyond his eighteenth birthday. At the end of his studies, I was told that he was one of the students who remained longest on their orphans' books, and his photograph alongside one of his dad's appeared in their newsletter. The article titled 'Fund helps Met Orphan achieve a dream' stated:

> *The son of an officer killed on duty has achieved his ambition to become a doctor. It was when he spent time in a hospital age eleven, that Michael decided that he wanted to train to be a doctor and thanks to the fund he was able to make a seemingly impossible dream come true.*

It was having the fearlessness to ask, seek and knock that opened doors that might have been otherwise closed. In the words of Jesus:

> And I say unto you, Ask and it shall be given to you, seek and ye shall find; knock, and it shall be opened to you. For everyone that asketh receiveth; and he that seeketh findeth; and to him that knocketh it shall be opened.
>
> LUKE 11: 9-10 (HOLY BIBLE).

I cannot forget the kindness I was shown and the help I was given through the rough and perilous times. I have a heart of gratitude for God's unending grace and for those who stood shoulder to shoulder with us.

One day during 2001 I received a surprise letter. The letter was an invitation from the Metropolitan Police to attend a special ceremony in remembrance of officers who had lost their lives in the line of duty. This recognition came thirty years after my husband's death. It was at this ceremony that I met Queen Elizabeth II and Ken Livingstone who was, at the time, the Mayor of London. A garden was located at the Police Training Academy for officers during this solemn occasion. It was then that a book of remembrance was opened and my husband's name was inscribed there. The inscription read, LESS WE FORGET: IN MEMORY OF THOSE OFFICERS WHO LOST THEIR LIVES IN THE LINE OF DUTY. The details of my husband's death were written in the book, which was presided over and opened by Queen Elizabeth II.

In memory of
M.E.D.L. Ince.

In later years I met Prince Charles and two Commissioners of Police, the most recent being Dame Cressida Dick. On the day when I met the Commissioner, I was invited to speak at a well-being event about how I had overcome trauma. It was the first time I had spoken in a public arena about my experience. It was after seeing the impact that it had on the participants and listening to their verbal feedback that I was finally inspired to write my story as it was *The Hard Truth*. I had resisted telling my story until I realised that it is not where you come from but where you end up that really matters. Who would have thought that I would be standing shoulder to shoulder with the Commissioner of Police?

105

By this time in my life I had accomplished many things, yet I saw this occasion as a sobering moment, given where I was in 1971.

Personal Reflections

Growing out of adversity is a slow process but I have discovered that adaptation to one's circumstances is the first step in turning tragedy around. Resilience comes after adversity, and in time leads to healing and eventually recovery. Resilience is not an inbuilt gene that is inherited at birth. It develops over time. It comes as a result of experiencing difficulties and as we develop strategies to cope and adjust to the problems we face. It may seem initially as if there is no way out, but with looking and searching for ways out of distressing situations we find the solutions. If you can keep moving forward taking one step at a time, your healing will be assured and you can look forward to brighter tomorrows.

Resilience developed as I looked forward, kept moving, kept smiling and as I made efforts to overcome against a backdrop of devastating and bewildering experiences. One of the gifts I was blessed with was the ability to laugh and oddly enough, I had a cheerful countenance, so that many people did not know the suffering I was experiencing. It was only as I voiced my feelings that people became aware of my predicament. The tools I utilised came from within and not from outside of me.

Resilience can be challenging when memories come as a powerful evocation of the past enacted through our senses. I have discovered that the more we engage with our five senses the more we are able to reach better outcomes. We can become resilient by refusing to dwell on the negatives and by focusing on positive things, which include forgiveness, focusing on spiritual growth, and developing new purpose and a new vision. This is where we gain perspective and transformation.

Finding meaning out of adversity is particularly difficult. Nevertheless, the meaning I drew from my adversity was to learn from defeat and when I was most vulnerable, I found ways to help and to be of service to others. This is one of the principles that led to my success after trauma. A point came in my life, when I stopped focusing on my tragedy and I turned my thoughts to others. This way of dealing with a traumatic experience became the strategy that gave me new vision, purpose and hopefulness. There are many resilient enhancing factors, but it was my spiritual centre that gave me freedom to move forward with new confidence and renewed hope.

Resilience develops as we look for ways to serve others. Service requires sacrifice and dedication. I was recently approached to teach students at very short notice. The designated lecturer was given leave of absence to complete his PhD and the person who had agreed to take the class could no longer meet this commitment. It was the final module and the students were hoping to graduate. The remuneration was significantly lower than I would earn in the normal course of my work. To add to matters, the university was a considerable distance from my home and involved a huge time commitment both in terms of preparation, teaching and travelling. I went the extra mile because that is what service demanded. In going the extra mile, I found that the service I rendered had a lasting positive impact since the students were able to graduate. It was the act of selfless service that helped the university to achieve an important milestone in meeting their promised obligations.

Resilience is built on survival strategies that allow us to adapt to unfavourable life events and circumstances. It is impossible to be protected from all the negative events that happen in life, but it is certain that we can help others to deal with the aftermath of negative experiences. These factors include providing a sense of direction, being hopeful, being proactive and building on one's strengths. Such strategies will enable us to look to the future with optimism.

Mike became resilient by osmosis, he watched how I behaved and he copied what he saw. Many people thought that he was not affected by the loss simply because he had not known his dad but this was far from the truth. He experienced the loss in a different way from myself. At times when I spoke to him and told him stories of his dad, he said that at school his peers would ask him why he did not have a dad. It was at times like these that he felt the loss but he did not speak of it, neither did he show bitterness. It seemed that it was just the way things were and he accepted it. As I was writing my memoir, I spoke to him about what it meant not to have a father around him. His response was thus:

> *I have no doubt that I had a deep resilience, I think I inherited and observed it from you. The secret of my success was that I had the capacity to absorb the pain and not let it stop me, I had to dig deep.*

Below I outline the five strategies that were most helpful as I began the long journey to recovery in order to grow out of adversity. The overarching theme was to live one day at a time and not rush into situations that could have long-term consequences. For example, refusing to remarry or settle with a partner as a result of loneliness was avoided. Instead, I relied on God to guide me through the dark days. Paul the Apostle said that faith without works is dead (James 2:17); therefore, I looked for personal resources from within and took action where it was possible. Finding resources from within was a key strategy for growing. It was possible to seek new direction as a way of moving forward. I gained strength to stay with the pain as I learnt how to become resilient. I was fortunate to be offered different types of support. As I recognised the need for help, I became responsive to accepting genuine forms of support, particularly when I could see that they would help us to move out of the circumstances that were created by misfortune.

Adopting a positive mindset during the most difficult times was transformational. Transformation comes by renewing one's mind and by thinking in new and different ways. Yet, this did not mean that the truth that was based on my experience had changed, but it meant that a positive way of thinking changed the dynamics of adversity and provided a new reality. It was a long time before I could reflect on the past, but when I did, it enabled me to put the past behind me and look to the future with optimism. These strategies are contained within what I term as the Five Rs of growing out of adversity.

1. Reliance: I relied on God to do things for me that I could not do for myself. Our best efforts can fail, but when we place our hand in the hand of God, He will allow us to experience newness of life and new beginnings. In our human relationships the notion of reliance is about trusting others to come through for us. It is when we know that a person can deliver what we need that helps us to cope. Equally, learning to let go and trust God brings calm and reassurance when everything else is chaotic and when it feels as if you are in a turbulent storm. Trusting also allows stress and worry to recede into the background.

2. Resourcefulness: I noticed that I became resourceful. This meant using existing resources within myself as a capacity builder to defeat limiting beliefs. Get to know your strengths and you will discover your resources. Complete an analysis known as a SWOT (Strengths, Weaknesses, Opportunities, Threats). Think about your strengths and play to them. We all have weaknesses, therefore in your analysis do not be afraid to identify your weaknesses or areas for personal growth. Look for new opportunities to strengthen your existing capacities. Opportunities come in different ways, but it is easy to overlook them when you are overwhelmed with grief. Therefore, do not allow opportunities to pass by because they may not come back again. Finally, assess any threats that might get in the way of your recovery. A threat could come in the form of stress, depression, anxiety, fear, self-doubt or a lack of confidence and motivation.

You will be surprised at what you will discover by completing your SWOT analysis. Being resourceful means digging deep and being intentional about personal growth. As Maxwell (2012) discovered personal growth is intentional and it is a process that takes time.

3. Redirection: I began by plotting a new path and setting out a new direction. It meant being proactive, and it also meant being in control of my thoughts, actions and behaviour. Notice your thoughts and moderate your behaviour. Choose a new path by reconstructing a new future. This new direction may or may not include people who are already in your life or it may involve searching for new friends by socialising and interacting with others. Remember that the foundation for redirection is your mindset. Therefore, direct your mind to focus on what you want to happen rather than what you do not want to happen.

4. Resilience: This is the strategy that will turn your life around and produce the outcome that you want. Resilience is the ability to bounce back from adversity after a traumatic loss. Be optimistic in your outlook, believing that any suffering you might be experiencing will not last forever. You will experience a turning-point. Stay around people who are positive and learn from them. Remember that if an eagle remains on the ground and fails to use his wings, he will never have the confidence to soar and become what he is intended to be. Paul the Apostle states that there are many benefits arising out of adversity that ultimately lead to resilience. Among these factors are peace, hope, patience and experiences that we can share with others even as we are going through adversity. Romans 5:1-5 (HOLY BIBLE)

5. Reflection: The process of reflection is a helpful strategy for coping with emotional issues that you may not feel able to speak about to others. It is cathartic to express your feelings by using a journal to record your innermost thoughts, feelings and

reactions. You can use your five senses, by calling forth memories that rely on your vision, hearing, smell, taste and feelings. For example, if you had a habit of going to a specific restaurant with a loved one or a friend, you would see the locality, hear the sounds in the restaurant, smell the food or the perfume you were wearing, as well as the feelings you experienced during those times. Using your imagination, you can brighten or dim the experience to make it into what you want it to be. It is about making sense of your experience. The next stage is to evaluate your experience and give it meaning. Out of this meaning you will decide on a plan which is very important because the plan determines the steps you will take to redirect and make transitional changes. In time you will go back to the situation that you thought was difficult, and you will say I cannot believe how far I have come. Regularly record your accomplishments and how you achieved them.

CHAPTER EIGHT

Studying: The Next Big Step

Moving along the upward spiral requires us to learn, commit and do on increasingly higher planes. We deceive ourselves if we think that any one of these is sufficient. To keep progressing, we must learn, commit and do, learn, commit, and do and learn, commit, and do again.

STEPHEN R COVEY: 1989

Turning tragedy around requires the ability to ask for what you need, it means seeking to knock on doors that may appear to be otherwise closed. It requires commitment, it requires taking action as well as putting the lessons learnt into practice. After all, this is the learning I took from my mother. There were many instances where the path to success required thinking less of my own resources and it was more about relying on God's limitless resources. My recovery began with the inner desire to change the course of events that came into my path with increasing momentum. Therefore, a momentous decision was required that equalled the task that would create change.

Turning my circumstances around began when I decided to study so that I could become self-supporting. This was when I began to grow, not for the sake of others but for personal development and fulfilment. It would take time but I was prepared to wait. I knew that if I could succeed in some form of dedicated study it would make up for the losses I had experienced in my early education. The hard truth was that standing still was not an option I could entertain. I developed a desire and an insatiable urge to grow.

I did not want to live on welfare benefit or become dependent on the state to give me handouts. One of the lessons my husband had taught me was not to rely on others to do things for me that I could do perfectly well for myself. I can thank him posthumously for his advice and guidance.

I wanted a measure of independence, therefore I took driving lessons and passed. It is unbelievable that during the early 1970s the cost of driving lessons was a mere ten shillings which in today's money would be approximately 50 pence. It is nostalgic even thinking about it. This simple action of taking my test and passing gave me the feeling of succeeding at something. I was the first of my sisters to achieve this goal. I already had my husband's car; therefore, I was set to take to the highways and byways. Investing in myself and looking to the future, even though it appeared bleak and uncertain, was the only way to go.

The next challenge was more psychological in nature because it required me to remove some of the barriers I had experienced as a child. To do so was the promise of mental freedom. In short, I had to create within myself the motivation to study so that I could improve my status by creating an avenue to gain earning power. I saw studying as a conduit to change. In his book, Rob Yeung (2012) states that change is only possible when we want it. Further, he contends that 'the more individualised our list of reasons for change, the more likely we may be to stay on track.'

I shifted my mindset from the idea that I wanted to follow my sisters into nursing. Instead, I wanted to create my own path and become a leader. There were few black people entering the profession of social work during those early years. I could see that there were opportunities to make my mark because I had the life experiences that would allow me to identify with other people's pain points. I registered at the local college for a one-year course in shorthand and typing in preparation for the next big challenge. A part-time course was better suited to my circumstances. Thus, I completed this year-long course while Mike attended the nursery on the grounds of the college. It was a timely provision that included parents wanting to improve themselves. I was in a class of teenage students who were naturally progressing from school and were on a career path. Once again, I felt awkward, but I persevered and did not quit.

I am reminded of Admiral William H. McRaven's address to Class 2014 at the University of Texas, Austin. He told the story of the training of the United States Navy SEALs. The recruits were put through rigorous training, but they were told that if they wanted a way out, they could ring a bell that stood in the courtyard. At all hours of the night the bell could be heard as the men were exhausted and too tired to bear the insurmountable pressure. Nevertheless, his advice was thus: do not ring the bell. It was only those who resisted ringing the bell who became successful.

At the end of this course, I got a job in a social work office as a typist. I did not particularly like the job but it opened my eyes to the social conditions of families and the hardships they were facing. I listened to social workers discussing their cases in an open- plan office. They communicated about many issues related to child abuse, removing children at risk from their families, mental health, disability, and problems affecting the elderly.

I was unaware of it, but the typing job placed me in a unique position to work in a professional setting, with the opportunity to observe what social workers were doing. It was from that vantage point that the vision to create change in my life became a reality. It created within me a new desire, and more specifically, a new purpose. The question was how I would get from where I was to where I now wanted to be. I could only do this by taking one small step at a time. One thing I knew for sure was that I did not want to become dependent on anyone. I wanted to make it on my own through personal effort and hard work. I took the next small step, went to college during the evening and gained good grades. It was this decision that brought light to my dark path. The belief that I could not achieve was forever challenged when I worked towards achieving the goal of passing the same examinations I had failed at school. Success means nothing unless we experience failure.

In the classic book, *Success Through a Positive Mental Attitude* by Napoleon Hill and Clement Stone (1987), they provide seventeen principles as the starting point for success. Of these principles there were three that captured my attention. The first is to develop 'definiteness of purpose' which is the starting point for all subsequent successes. The second is to take 'personal initiative'. Application of this principle allowed me to take action. The third principle I needed to apply was 'self-discipline'. Later on, the other principles followed and became active. Along with their advice that a person's life could change if they recognised that they had the power to change their direction, this was a revelation to me. It was a light bulb moment. I could make change happen if I so desired.

My Christian teaching allowed me to know that God had a superior vision and purpose for my life if I only could trust and believe in His power to turn around my life. Solomon wrote:

> Trust in the Lord with all thine heart; and lean not unto thine own understanding. In all thy ways acknowledge Him, and he shall direct thy paths.
>
> PROVERBS 3: 5-6 (HOLY BIBLE).

I was depending on God to show me how to achieve the vision that was created in my mind. Thus, I began to pray earnestly for help to achieve my goal. It is said in the Scriptures that we must ask, seek and knock. I would have to do a lot of asking, knocking and seeking to overcome insurmountable hurdles and barriers, some in my mind and others outside of my mind. The principles that Hill and Stone proposed became my driver.

When we want to achieve any goal, it is critical to not only visualise it, but moreover to take action. Thus, my first action step involved returning to college to gain the certificates that drew me nearer to my goal. Again, motivation, perseverance, aspiration and insight were required to make the leap. Having achieved good results, I felt ready to tackle a more demanding course of study. I applied to The Open University to begin a BA degree in psychology. My thinking at this time was that I wanted to counsel the bereaved and people experiencing social problems.

After I had completed the first year of the Bachelor's degree in psychology, I finally decided that I wanted to become a social worker. I wasted no time and applied to the local college of Higher Education.

Evidently the course leaders did not have the same time frame as myself in mind. They told me to reapply one year later when I would, in their estimation, magically reach maturity. In their view I needed to be slightly older and wiser. The truth of it was that they were unaware of my history and that I probably had more experience than most students applying to undertake that course of study. The requirement was to sit a psychometric test, which would involve some form of maths. Maths was not my favourite subject, but I had determined in my mind that it was the course I wanted to complete; thus, I was prepared to take the test. On the day I arrived at the college, there was a technical problem which meant that the psychometric test was abandoned. In its place, my assignment was to write an essay. Well, I was much better at writing and by God's mercies I passed and was accepted onto the three-year part-time course in 1979. This was eight years after my bereavement. On the first day of the course, I told the tutors that I was nearing the end of the first year of the Psychology degree. They appeared amazed but immediately said that it would be too taxing to complete two courses of study at the same time. Hence, I made the decision to abandon the Psychology degree and, in its place, completed the social work course. I believed that the latter would lead to employment and I was correct in my thinking. Psychology was a part of the social work curriculum; thus, I was able to continue my interest in that subject.

I did not know where this path would lead me, but it felt like a challenge and herein my life was on the verge of a breakthrough. I began to prepare for my course and during the summer months I read a classic book titled *Dibs in Search of Self*. It was a book that brought awareness to me about the plight of an abused child. I wept as I read it and decided that I wanted to help children who had suffered from the impact of abuse. This area of social work became the cause for which I would later stand up, and it became my way of teaching others how to care for vulnerable children.

At this time and while I was studying, Mike was attending junior school. Mama was instrumental in the support she gave that allowed me time to study and successfully complete my course over a period of three years.

Personal Reflections

In my work as a life coach, I have met many individuals who wanted to become successful but gave up because they became disillusioned or because they prioritised other things. People who are successful do not quit, but they will face every challenge, and fight every battle to realise their dream.

On reflection, I know that successful people are introspective because they look inside of themselves rather than looking to others or blaming others for their failure. They are driven by a sense of urgency and with a deep desire to make every action count. They are able to visualise their dream and turn it into reality. They are unbelievably passionate, gathering momentum minute by minute, day after day, year in year out. They set goals with a realistic time frame and work to reach deadlines. I believe that successful people do not only promote themselves, but the bottom line is that they promote others. This thinking was at the centre of what I dared to become.

Returning to education as an adult learner has two perspectives. An adult learner might feel that they are at a disadvantage because they may have family and other commitments that would impinge on the time they have to study. Thus, the level of commitment might not be high and it would take a high level of motivation to engage with a programme of study and all it demands. For those with an experience of failure and setbacks in their basic education, returning to advanced studies would present a challenge. There could also be relationship problem when one partner wants to study and the other is uninterested or feels threatened by their partner's new-found knowledge and enlightenment. The second perspective is that it could be seen as a distinct advantage for those adults who want to create a new path for themselves. The vision of attaining a long-held dream, preparing for a career and personal achievement, is both rewarding and satisfying. From this vantage point, the impetus to study and to gain knowledge is a step towards upward mobility. Learning new ideas is also about making a conscious choice to promote one's self, advance and make new discoveries. I was able to use education in later life as a stepping stone to better ways of knowing. Therefore, I engaged with the second perspective in my quest to learn and develop.

CHAPTER NINE

Following My Passion

Your reason and your passion are the rudder and sails of your seafaring soul. If either your sails or your rudder be broken, you can but toss and drift, or else be held at a standstill in mid-seas.

(KAHLIL GIBRAN, 1980 P.59)

I first became aware that I had a gift for teaching, and moreover public speaking, when I was training to become a social worker. One of the assignments was to deliver a presentation on a topic we had studied throughout the semester. I prepared well and when I finished the presentation there was loud applause. Approval was equally reflected in the verbal feedback I immediately received. My peers were impressed and this was reflected in their animation and affirmation. After the presentation one of my peers turned to me and said, 'I was so nervous, how did you do that?'. I turned to her in utter amazement and said, 'Do what?'. She did not know that my heart was racing like a trotting horse, but despite my nervousness, I managed to complete the presentation. It was this first presentation that set me out as a leader among the students. I successfully qualified in 1982 and the world was my oyster.

I met the first white woman on this course with whom I developed a friendship that was not superficial. As our friendship grew, she often referred to that presentation and would say to me that I had the ability to become a teacher. I often responded with surprise at her comments, but I never forgot her words of encouragement and clung onto them.

On controversial topics such as race, gender, discrimination, difference, disability and other social issues I was always willing to speak out because I detested injustice. I often raised issues concerning

119

discrimination and racism that other students felt too delicate a topic to approach. I fearlessly championed the cause of the underdog. Possibly because it was truly a part of my life experience. I knew what it felt like to be on the end of discrimination. In this area I was a thought-provoker. My fiery personality would not allow me to sit back and keep silent. Thinking back, I had this passion all along. I was not afraid to speak out, but somewhere along the line it was beaten out of me and of my own volition I had exchanged it for timidity. It was a time in my life when I was growing in self-confidence but I was not aware that I had the capacity to express my thoughts in a formal setting. My preference was to listen because I felt that others had more important things to say. However, I noticed that when I felt intensely passionate, I allowed my voice to be heard. Strangely enough, students and lecturers would listen to what I had to say. They admired my bravado and intrepid spirit. The ability to speak in an academic setting while being observed and scrutinised was the making of me. I felt empowered by this process. Nevertheless, as my career developed, I learnt that the ability to listen actively was the best form of communication. It became an invaluable skill when I became a life coach. I was able to listen to people and process their issues without interrupting, but knowing how to ask questions that would stimulate their thinking.

In reality my work-life began relatively late. I was thirty-one years old when I completed my training and was ready to move into the world of paid employment. It was an exciting time because I had grown along a continuum from being despondent to being hopeful about the future. Mike had finished junior school and was ready to move onto secondary school. This was an important transition that we were making together. Even though we were moving in different directions, there were hope, optimism and expectancy.

As Mike was preparing to begin his secondary education, I was beginning my first job as a qualified social worker. The Seventh-day Adventist Church where we were members graciously agreed to provide partial financial support to enable him to attend the church school as a weekly boarder. The school had a good reputation for successfully getting children through their examinations. My aspiration for Mike was that he should have every conceivable opportunity so that he would eventually reach the apex of the career he would eventually choose. I knew that he had potential, and I wanted him to have the opportunities I did not have as a child. Although it was our first time apart, it allowed both of us to find our wings while maintaining his stability. Carter Hodding's words are of great value because he said that:

> There are only two lasting bequests we can hope to give our children. One of these is roots; the other, wings'.
>
> (CARTER HODDING)

It was around the age of eleven years old when Mike told me that he wanted to choose medicine as his career. His decision was confirmed when he went into hospital for a minor operation. At the end of his stay, he reconfirmed his personal aspiration to me. Initially, I was disappointed because in my mind, I had his path mapped out, which was that he would become a concert pianist. It was evident that he had the ability to do so, but he was given decision-making power and personal choice to determine his path. I supported him in the choice he made and relegated music as his hobby. I was willing to work hard, and to sacrifice my personal needs so that he could with time achieve his dream and ultimate goal.

Moving to boarding school brought an end to our relationship with Cathy, his music teacher. It was a sad ending because she had made a significant and positive impact on his mind during the most formative years of his development. She gave him positive input through music and it became an integral part of our lives. Many activities revolved around music bringing our home alive and making it vibrant.

After Mike had settled into his new school, I registered him at the local music school. This is where we met his second music teacher. His teacher,

Paula, was an older and gracious woman who had never married and who was dedicated to teaching music. She had an unmistakeable love for children and wanted to see them do well. She symbolically adopted an endless stream of children entering her room and her home. As with Cathy, we developed a good relationship with her. She liked Mike and called him 'Mr. Somebody' in a playful and teasing way along with a nudge in his side when he slipped up along the way, or did not practise as hard as she felt he was capable of doing. Her standards, expectations and ethics were high. We would laugh heartily at Paula's expressions and marvel at the depth of her knowledge as much as we would laugh at his mistakes. Mike did well under her tutelage and loving care. Similar to Cathy she felt that he was capable of developing a musical career and gave him plenty of encouragement.

Paula encouraged him to enter for competitions where he was able to achieve certificates and trophies along with constructive feedback. Students gathered at her home to listen to each other play. We did not miss any of these events. Mike spent five years at secondary school and graduated with several O-Level Certificates. He also achieved Grade 4 piano theory and Grades 5 and 8 practical with distinction. He was now ready to move forward and continue with advanced studies.

I was dedicated to his success and did everything that was within my power to assist him. I recall travelling to the school one evening each week after a long day's work to take him to his music lessons. It was an important developmental stage for him both in terms of his school life and his extracurricular activities. Taking this action reduced the time we were separated and kept our relationship strong.

At the end of secondary school Mike received excellent grades, but he wanted to return home and attend the local college to take his A-Levels. Unfortunately, the freedom and less structured way of teaching presented him with opportunities to be self-determining. Like most young people, he was in the position where he had to make the transition during this stage of his education. This change impacted negatively on his studies and he did not achieve the grades that he had hoped for to accept the place he was offered at medical school.

I could identify with him, because this was my experience when I left school. What I understood about my son the day he received his results was that he was blessed with a determined spirit. He threw an object on the ground and walking around it said convincingly, 'If I don't get it this way, then I will get it another way'. His demonstration showed that he was prepared to go all out to follow his passion. This gave me hope that he would reach his goal. I was prepared to work with him, and encouraged him by saying that if he did his best that would be good enough for me. This is where failure is turned around into success. What is important is not that we fail, but rather the extent to which we are willing to go in order to achieve a dream. It is often in failing that we succeed.

Mike returned to Sixth Form College at Cambridge and achieved even better grades than were expected for entry to medical school. He was accepted at two of the most prestigious medical schools in London, St Bartholomew's and University College Hospital. He chose the latter without realising that this was the hospital where his father had died. It was another remarkable coincidence or was it a part of a bigger plan that we did not see at the time? The stage was set for the next seven years of academic studies. Although I did not complete the Psychology degree, Mike achieved an intercalated BSc degree in Psychology during his medical studies. He began his work-life as a houseman, senior houseman and registrar. He decided to complete further studies to become a General Practitioner. In this he succeeded. From this point forward, nothing could stop him because his level of motivation was high.

Passion is an inner feeling that only comes alive when a person is committed to and convinced of a cause they believe in. It is the willingness to follow a path even when there are obstacles and challenges standing in the way. Passion comes alive when people are willing to stand up for what they believe. For me a cause must be worthy and I must have a deep conviction of the validity of any cause for which I am willing to fight. It is my passion that allowed me to defend what I feel in my heart of hearts to be right, fair and just. It must be a cause I am willing to fight for even against the odds.

The success of which I am about to write came from the passion that was burning in me. It came mostly from life experiences, from unfavourable circumstances, that were turned around. Success requires passion and invariably follows adversity and not the other way around. It can come early or late in life; it just depends on where we are at any given time and how we work to create successful outcomes. If I were to plot a graph, I would say that my success followed a certain trajectory with elements that formed a recurring pattern.

My first job as a social worker came directly after I qualified and Mike went to boarding school during the week, returning home at the weekend. It seemed like we always began a project in tandem, and there was something that was consistent about the way I plotted my aspirations alongside his without being in competition. This was the way our lives dovetailed. After graduating I was immediately offered a position as a basic-grade social worker. I had made it into the professional world with 'rooky' status. I had a long way to go and a lot to learn. I would need to graduate from the school of 'hard knocks' before I could claim to be an expert in my field of practice.

I find it hard to believe as I look back, but the position I first acquired was in a developmental role to work with people in the black and minority ethnic community. It was an area of interest I had developed during my training and I was keen to make my mark. However, the problem was that it was a poisoned chalice. It was a difficult role to play because there was no blueprint, no guidance and a lack of interest on the part of my colleagues in this work. It was not in the mainstream, but on the margins. At the same time, I had to develop my knowledge and skills within the social-work field. In essence, I was playing a double role. I found myself fighting to have my voice heard.

Creating a change in mindset within a large organisation required considerable boldness and perseverance. After two years of hitting my head against a brick wall I decided that it was time to move on. It was at my farewell party that the Director described me as a person with tenacity. It is odd how people only say the things that really matter when it is too late, by which time you are moving on, and they applaud you in a valedictory speech. Nevertheless, I carried the meaning of that word with me for a long time because it appeared to say something important about my personality. It means to be persistent, to have determination, drive and steadfastness. This sentiment came as a revelation as I had never imagined that I was held in such high esteem in his mind, or moreover, that I possessed such qualities. I had to be explicitly told and reminded.

Making the decision to move turned out to be a wise one. I had moved to a specialist position in an adoption and fostering team. This was the area where many years later I would build my freelance and consultancy business.

My job was to work with three others to set up a fostering team. The team was to focus on recruiting foster carers to look after black children who had been placed in residential homes in locations far away from their families. It was the first time I had worked in an all-female team and it was a wonderful experience.

As the children came to visit the unit, I noticed a distinct lack of identity and self-pride. It reminded me of some of my early experiences as a child. I was lost for words when one of the boys referred to the black members of the team in derogatory ways. I became curious and disturbed at his language and negative way of describing black people like himself. Identity confusion is when a person rejects who they are in preference to assuming an alternative identity. They adopt an identity that is not their own, thriving on the belief that to do so is more attractive and desirable. They hold onto the belief that they will be accepted by the dominant group. This is an erroneous belief because they must give up their identity in order to fit in and be accepted. There is always a price to be paid for the things we want whether positive or negative. In order to understand this phenomenon, I researched the impact of trans-racial adoption and fostering and found it to be a common phenomenon among black children, particularly those who were separated from family and community.

While I was working in the specialist fostering team, one of the team members saw an advertisement for a Team Leader in an inner-city area. She approached me saying, 'Lynda you should apply for this job because I have seen that you have the skills to be a leader'. I was apprehensive, but as she would not take no for an answer, I applied and was successful. It is strange what people notice, but it is about how you carry yourself and how you apply your ethics.

On my first day I arrived early and as I was sitting in my office, I heard two members of the team talking as they approached my door. Not knowing that I had already arrived, I heard one of them saying, 'Let us see how long she will last on this ship.' I knew from the outset that there was an expectation of failure or else they would ensure that I did not succeed. It was imperative that on this ship I needed my rudder and sails to remain firmly in place. I needed to be in control of the direction in which the ship was going.

I was positioned in a leadership role with the prospect of moving up the managerial ladder. Sounds good, but it was a tough job. I was leading a wayward team with little interest in being conscientious and without a sense of the work ethic. During team meetings they fought me at every turn, refusing to take the cases I allocated to them. They arrived on time and left on time. No one could accuse them of not working the hours for which they were paid. I was often alone in the office making sure that what they did not do, I did. It was this first entry-level of leadership that became my testing ground. It was an unsafe environment in which I was working. It was not only the volume of complex child protection cases that called for absolute vigilance and focus, but the resentment of team members that was harrowing. I had to cover my back, be on guard and watch out for the pitfalls they consistently set for me. It was out of this experience that I was tested, some days beyond endurance. Yet, the difficulties I experienced on this battle ground became my learning ground as I was forced to sharpen my skills. To become a successful leader, I would need to forget the title, roll up my sleeves and lead by example. Success is possible if we are willing and able to set goals and work systematically at achieving them with a positive mental attitude. Passion is the name of the game because that is what kept me going and made life attractive, it kept me striving for the next goal.

There is a story about two men who were asked to chop down some trees in a forest. The older man would stop intermittently to sharpen his saw, while the young man carried on working feverishly. At the end of the contest the older man won. The younger man was mystified and asked how it was possible for the older man to win when he constantly rested. He was told that the older man did it by taking time to sharpen his saw. This is what I did; I took time to reflect and to learn from what was going on around me.

I arrived in the office early and left later than every other team member. I became observant and hyper-vigilant. Their intention was to prove that I was only given the job because of positive discrimination. This would justify their position in believing that I was chosen for the job based on protected characteristics rather than qualifications, experience and merit. Thus, I was placed in a position where I had to maintain mental focus, deal with inevitable hurdles and remain watchful to prove my opponents wrong. It was at this stage that I asked myself some pertinent questions. Getting into the 'what, when, where and how' frame of mind, I asked: what is your dream? when will your dream be realised? how will you achieve your dream? In other words, what would be the methodology and the process? One of the most important questions was, where would the strength come from to achieve my dream? These were questions that I could not answer immediately but it was only with the passing of time that each was answered in a way that gave me direction and the certainty that I was searching for success, not necessarily in terms of money, but in terms of ethics, knowledge, skills and best practice.

In moving to a job that I thought held much attraction for me, I moved along a continuum of disillusionment and moreover defeat. I struggled to work in an arena dominated by white males. This was an unusual phenomenon because social work is more often than not a female-dominated profession. However, I found that it was not so much about gender as it was about race and limited expectations linked to old ideas of superiority and inferiority. The idea that there is a glass ceiling and that only certain people cannot break through it, challenged my dream and often had a devastating impact on my thinking. It is the way we think that is the prelude to our failure or success. If I was going to make it, then I had to jettison the negative thoughts, replacing them with a more positive outlook.

Two of the male members of the team I was leading had applied for the same position but were unsuccessful. It appeared that there was conflict between senior managers and team members. It also appeared that the senior managers were either incapable of or unwilling to challenge the behaviours of team members because they were vociferous and self-assured. They hid behind each other with unrelenting commitment. As a new member of the team, I was the outsider, hence they used psychological bullying tactics against me, which I must admit made me afraid. It was like nothing I had seen before; it was a new level of harassment. The quintessential question they asked was whether I supported them as a cohesive team or rather the senior managers. I refused to rise to their bait or to take sides, thus my obstinacy resulted in exclusion. Failure to get on the other side also resulted in isolation. In their minds, I became a threat, an interloper and someone they could not trust. Hence, they wittingly planned my demise. Their behaviour was motivated by two of the most powerful human emotions, fear and jealousy.

It was when I was feeling sorry for myself that a glimmer of hope appeared on the horizon and answered my first question, 'what is your dream?'. But it did not come without testing. We not only learn by our own intentions but through the intentions and goodwill of others. I was able to answer the first question when another person who had the title of a Race Relations Officer sensed my distress and proposed a meeting with senior managers and the team. I had been fastidious in collecting evidence and prepared well for the meeting with my adversaries. It was through his coaching that I was able to see that I could rise to the demands of the job and that out of it I could realise my dream to reach the next stage of my career. I realised that all the resources I needed were inside of me. All I needed to do was to be confident and act it out in practical ways.

One of the truths of my life is that when I have felt weakest is when I have been made strong, not in my strength but through God's strength. Paul the Apostle wrote:

> And he said to me, my grace is sufficient for thee: For my strength is made perfect in weakness.
>
> 2 CORINTHIANS 12:9 (HOLY BIBLE).

It is an anomaly, but I had to become weak before I could be convinced that I had the capacity to be a strong leader.

On the day of the meeting, the entire team sat in a circle and the meeting was presided over by the Area Manager and the Race Relations Officer. As I read out from my script the behaviours of the team members there was strong denial and counter-denial. Suddenly ground shifted as grown men began crying. One of their chief protagonists did not arrive for work the next day. With a weakening of their position two others resigned, leaving the way clear to recruit new members to the team. However, the bullying did not stop because as new members were recruited their minds were poisoned. The change came when I was jointly interviewing a client in a closed room. Without provocation or warning she picked up a phone that was hanging on the wall and assaulted me in my face, narrowly missing my right eye. I stood up in indignation but my manager told me to sit down. When I returned to the team, they were angry about how a senior manager had handled this situation. Instantly their attitude changed towards me.

Two years after this incident I saw an advertisement to fill a similar post nearer to my home. It was the breakthrough I desired. I had many questions and thoughts about making a move, but I prayed about it for several days. My prayer was simple and uncomplicated. I asked God to give me a sign. Three days before the closing date I had a premonition that I should complete the application form. I felt the urge to take action. Hence, at the eleventh hour I decided to throw caution to the wind, I completed the form and applied not thinking that I would be called for an interview. It was a measure of faith that allowed me to take this action.

Several days later I received a letter inviting me for an interview. I greeted it with surprise, and great anticipation. I was offered the position of team leader in an interdisciplinary team. It was one of the most rewarding and happiest experiences of my career for the next seven years. Reputation is a very important aspect of a person's professionalism, so it was with relative ease that I had developed my reputation by expanding my knowledge and building positive work relationships. A person cannot buy reputation because it is part of a value system they develop and it becomes a part of their character. It is true that there is no lack of people wanting to be leaders but a real lack of people who are authoritative and authentic leaders.

It was at this stage that I was able to answer the second question. When do you want to achieve your dream? I realised that there was no time like the present. Thinking of the role I occupied I wanted to be a good and effective leader in the present. Kouzes and Posner (2017) posit that there are five truths about exemplary leadership. These are not the only truths, but they impress me as critical to becoming a successful leader. The first is to be able to influence others; the second is to create trust, credibility and integrity. The third is to demonstrate a set of values and beliefs that guide a leader's intentions. The fourth is to have vision. The fifth is that leaders experience failure before success. John Maxwell (2017) also offers some sound advice about leadership. He states that a good leader focuses on 'making people, starting people and growing people.' Wherever my journey would lead, from this point forward developing people would become my mantra, my purpose and my passion.

A Change In Direction

Life is an endless stream of changes. In fact, the only certainty we have in life is that it will change, yet we can resist change because it feels good to remain in our comfort zone. It is much better to get into a stretch zone where it is possible to develop the capacity to build on what we already know. The psychologist Robert Yeung studied change from a scientific perspective. He mentions two regulatory orientations. One is related to the benefits change will bring and the other considers the risks involved. Both are valid ways of bringing about change but they have different outcomes. He concludes that:

> The more people understand themselves and their orientations in life, the more they tend to succeed in their goals.
>
> (YEUNG, R. 2012)

As I had settled into my position and felt comfortable, my comfort zone was to be tested. It came in the form of major organisational changes and I would need to adjust and make preparations for moving on. This re-organisation required all team leaders to re-apply for their positions. Some jobs would be deleted, meaning that some people would be made redundant or demoted. As was my strategy, I prepared weeks in advance and built up my confidence for the interview and the process I was to go through. Another team leader, who was a new member of staff, and I were placed in the uncomfortable position where we had to apply for the same job. After the interview, I emerged from a barrage of questions; I was offered a new position as a manager.

My opposite number was demoted. When we both returned to the office and announced the news, commiserations were showered upon my opponent and no congratulations were offered to me.

Realising that the team secretly favoured my colleague, I was dumbfounded. To put it bluntly, I was now in a position where I would have to gather strength to manage a team in a climate of discontent. To be placed in this position was not by choice, it was a change that was declared to be outside of my control. During the transitional period we were working with the certain knowledge that my colleague's days were numbered and that she would be drafted into another team. My biggest question of self-inquiry was how I would overcome this impasse. My strategy was to 'act as if' it had not happened. The concept of 'acting as if' is when a person acts as if they had already achieved a goal they are pursuing. It is a strategy that refutes doubt and gives a broad base of self-belief, to challenge and repudiate feelings of fear and doubt that can lead to overwhelm. In his book *Pursuit of Happyness*, Chris Gardner (2006) tells a story of when he asked his mother for money. She told him to act as if he already had it. It was a lesson he never forgot.

The hard truth was that I had to confess to God that I was overwhelmed because I had the distinct feeling of being deflated like a balloon. I felt let down by the duplicity of people I had trusted. For several months there was an undercurrent in the office and I dreaded going into work where I was forced to face and contend with my colleagues.

Before preparing to leave my home for work I would sit and rehearse the words I wanted to say with exactitude, but in situations where I had to address my colleagues, and in meetings, I found it difficult to articulate my thoughts and words. I felt as if the eyes of others were focused on me and it inhibited my expressions. This was the enemy called fear. It was a repeat of what I had experienced at school and it came back to haunt me. It became stressful to operate in this hostile environment or even to exercise my authority. I must confess that I was near to breaking-point and the edge of discouragement. I was feeling like a failure even when in reality I had been successful. I called on friends for support and I was told that I had to define my own expectations and not be led by the whims or feelings of others. They told me that I had to believe in myself if I wanted to make the transition. My mother told me that if God had placed me in that position His grace would be sufficient. She told me that when God opens a door no-one can close it. This meant that I could lead the team for as long as God willed it to be so, and as long as I had the determination and staying power to make it work. Armed with this advice I began to understand how I could change things around. The nature of my resilience was once again shown as a pattern I could follow to sustain my dream and bring it to fruition.

Once the team became resigned to the inevitable, life reverted to normality but I could not enjoy the comfort and ease of relationships I had previously relished. Life in the team changed. For that matter I had changed because I began to see that human nature is the same wherever you go. Although it is true that people are different, it struck me that the truth of it is that human nature is basically the same. If we want to overcome the wrongs that people have done to us, we must not only move on, but moreover, we must learn how to forgive so that negative feelings are not transferred to other people or other situations.

The concept of forgiveness freed me to move forward without regret and bitterness. I have discovered that the spirit of reconciliation has many benefits. The first is that it is a buffer against negative emotions that can be soul-destroying. Feelings of animosity that could cripple and keep a person in a vice-like grip of hate and revenge can be dispelled through the act of forgiveness. It was the concept of forgiveness that helped me to shift my thinking and to open up the channels of communication. I recognised that working in partnership and in collaboration would have a better outcome if not immediately, then for future good relations.

The positive of forgiveness is how it gives freedom to move on with one's life without feeling weighed down by negative feelings, resentment and bitterness. Rising above injustice is also a key factor in the healing process. The life of Christ is a perfect example of how forgiveness works by bringing calm to troubling situations. I believe that forgiveness is not an easy thing to do, but it is the only thing to do if we are seeking for meaning in our adversity, for a solution and for renewal.

Dreams have a way of being distorted; they begin and may never end, unless we create a focus and use the insight that is given as a turning-point to our advantage. During this time there were four strategies that provided a way of escape and kept me holding on so that I was able to achieve my dream.

The first strategy was to exercise faith. Faith is not based on evidence, it is not seen, but we experience it as we see answers to our prayers and petitions. Faith worked wonders for me because it increased my reliance on God and less on what I was humanly able to accomplish. It has always been the hallmark of my success. Here is an example of how faith helped me to overcome disappointment. I was working in an environment where my colleagues were constantly complaining; their mindset was focused on all the bad that had been created by change. I was tempted to believe that nothing would change. I exchanged this way of thinking through prayer and meditation, which gave me clarity of thought. I used a few moments every morning to meditate on a thought for the day and a verse of Scripture. I started to believe that the day had something good in store for me. It was this type of consistency that eventually took me to a different plateau. Being intentional also creates a faith perspective and brings the things we are asking for to fruition. Thus, there is an undeniable connection between the mind [thoughts], feelings and actions.

The second was to develop an attitude of gratitude; it is a chain breaker, so that even when each chain of events looked bleak, I gave thanks. It is easy to give thanks when everything is going well, but what about when life presents trials and difficulties? This is the time to give thanks. Long before I became a life coach, I had developed the habit of keeping a gratitude journal. This activity has served me well over the years as it has become a daily focus. I have learnt the importance of expressing gratitude each day. I may feel on some days that nothing out of the ordinary has happened, but I do not look for the big things, rather I look for the small and insignificant things that make up the mosaic pattern of life, making it meaningful. A close friend of mine has been going through a difficult time because her husband has been suffering with cancer. She did not claim to be a Christian, but she knew that I had a strong faith and that I was praying for God to touch and heal her husband. Recently, she called and as she talked about how this disease had taken over her life. I sensed that she did not want pity, so she said, 'We still have a lot to be thankful for'. I agreed because even in our darkest hour we can still give thanks. Accordingly, Mark T. Mitchell Professor of Political Science at Patrick Henry College in Virginia writes:

> *Gratitude is born of humility, for it acknowledges the giftedness of the creation and the benevolence of the Creator. ... The humble person says that life is a gift to be grateful for, not a right to be claimed. Humility ushers in a grateful response to life.*

Third, was to surround myself with people who could give positive advice and with whom I could share my knowledge, expertise and experience. When I was invited to speak on topics of interest, I accepted because it gave me a platform to share knowledge and increase the contribution I was making to social-work practice.

The fourth was to read literature that gave inspiration and encouragement. In the book written by Dickens and Dickens (1991) some helpful advice is given to black managers based on solution-focused concepts. I found it particularly helpful to know that within the professional domain it is important to deal with facts and not emotions. Dealing with facts helps with gaining clarity and seeing the world from different perspectives and viewpoints. An important concept I drew from this book was the importance of identifying my adversaries, supporters and inner resources.

Based on this advice I began to think about the gifts I already had and how I could strengthen my position. Having information to hand when it was needed gave the impression that I was a resource and a specialist within my own area of practice. This gave me leverage and a strong position from which to stake a claim for leadership. Within my personality was a trait called generosity. I discovered that generously sharing my skills and knowledge was opening a window of opportunity not just for others but moreover for me. The more I gave, the more was returned to me in ways that I did not understand or expect.

Wintley Phipps says that God has a way of making up for every deficit we experience. He states with a strong conviction that:

> It is in the quiet crucible of your personal private sufferings that your noblest dreams are born and God's greatest gifts are given in compensation for what you have been through.
>
> WINTLEY PHIPPS

The fifth strategy was to consistently meditate on God's word. This activity strengthened me inwardly. It was the devotional books that encouraged me to interpret and record my feelings and to offer every sad moment to the God who became my constant friend. Today, I look back at my journals and read copious notes that explained my innermost feelings, disappointments and fears, as well as my hopes.

Personal Reflections

Turning my life around called for a great deal of courage. To work and be self-supporting was at the heart of everything I wanted. Although stress in any work environment is inevitable it can also create an imbalance. I brought work home, and the consequence was a lack of clear division between my work and personal life. When we are overcome with stress it is difficult to see what is blatantly obvious. Stress kept my engine going to the point where I felt unable to step off the notorious treadmill. Each time I took annual leave I became ill. I was unable to create the balance I needed to replenish my batteries. On one occasion when I came out of the doors at work, I knew that there was a wall behind me. I got into my car and reversed into it. I did not realise that the balance had gone until I made an error of judgement. Balance is extremely important because we need to recognise the need to rest. This is why Jesus said:

> And he said unto them, Come ye yourselves apart and into a desert place and rest a while. For they were many coming and going, and they had no leisure so much as to eat.
>
> MARK 6:31 (HOLY BIBLE)

Work was an important part of my life but when I arrived home and closed the door, I had no-one to share the good and bad experiences with. I had little time for exercise or leisure. When we find ourselves tipping towards an unhealthy work-life balance the only sensible thing to do is to take stock.

Respect is earned, it calls for ethical values. It is not a right. As I reflect on some of my earliest memories of how I was raised, I keep retuning to the values that are very important to me. In thinking of the many disappointments in my career, I can honestly say that at the end of the day I was respected for the ethical stance I took as I worked alongside others and as I promoted fairness, transparency and non-discrimination. In this way I encouraged others to see that it does not matter what happens to us or who we are that matters, it is more to do with how we respond to the curveballs that are thrown at us. There is always a price to pay for the things we want out of life.

CHAPTER TEN
Breakthrough to Success

I know of no more encouraging fact than the unquestionable ability of man to elevate his life by conscious endeavour.

(HENRY DAVID THOREAU)

My life had changed to the point where I preferred to live rather than die. I have already stated that the hard truth is that we have no control over whether we live or die. However, we have control over the decisions we make and the endeavours we pursue. There are actions we can take to prolong our lives but, in the end, death is the one thing that we cannot control. Whether we are rich or poor, black or white, educated or uneducated, male or female, none of these human factors matter when it comes right down to the hard truth. The truth is that if we want to succeed at any endeavour, we must be proactive and being proactive means taking responsibility, making choices and acting from a position of strength. I pursued a course of action quietly and did not flaunt my achievements, but people noticed and celebrated my success at various stages of my career.

After two years in a new managerial role, I had two life experiences that allowed me to know that God had a purpose for my life and that I should not give up. The first came when Mama and I were travelling with a friend. I loved antiques and he agreed to drive us to an antiques show. The intention was to enjoy a day out. We were travelling along the M4 at a steady pace when suddenly one of the tyres of his car punctured. The car flipped and landed upside down. In the turn I saw the blue sky. I heard Mama in the back seat as she shouted 'God save us.' I recall the fear as we stood up and weaved our way out of the car. When we looked behind a huge juggernaut came to a screeching halt yard behind my friend's car. It was miracle because all three of us walked away virtually unscathed. We were taken to the nearest hospital but were not detained.

The second incident when my life was spared was when I was taken ill and required a hysterectomy. During the operation I had a near-death experience. In preparation for my operation, the medical staff made an error that placed my life in jeopardy. They administered warfarin, an anti-blood-clotting medication, but the dosage was too high. It was a day later that the signs of internal bleeding became evident. I needed to return to the operating table to stem the flow of blood. When I eventually gained consciousness, I had similar feelings to those I had experienced after the death of my husband and before I had given birth to my son. I felt as if the bed could not contain me and as if I was drifting out into space. I clung on for my life. It was six weeks before I was discharged. During this period of hospitalisation my mother, my son and youngest sister joy were constantly by my side giving support and willing me to live.

Mike was at the end of his school life and had returned home. He still firmly believed that becoming a doctor was his chosen path. He visited me as I lay on my sick bed he gave me a Bible verse of consolation. It said this:

> Humble yourselves, therefore, under the mighty hand of God, that he may exalt you in due season. Casting all your care upon Him; for he cares for you.
>
> 1 PETER 5:6-7 (HOLY BIBLE).

And He took care of my anxiety and gave me freedom from fear worry and anxiety. This was reassuring as I struggled for my life.

My recovery took three months and during this extended period of absence from my job, I sat for hours thinking and reflecting about what the future would hold for me. It was this change that gave me new vision. One of the things I reflected on was the positive feedback I had been consistently given about my teaching skills. When I returned to work, I found that the team's dynamics had changed and it felt as though I no longer belonged in that environment. I felt awkward and out of place. My colleagues showed no compassion but felt as if I had let them down by being sick. It was a crazy situation and it became a nightmare.

I am not sure whether it was noticed that I was unhappy, or that I had become a misfit, or whether someone was earmarked for my job, but not long after I had returned to work the senior manager summoned me into his office. He told me that he was aware of my interest in training. He advised me that I could seek to move to the training department. A three-way meeting was arranged with a representative from the training department. It was during this meeting that the representative suggested that I could update my training in preparation for a possible smooth transition. A sideways move was how it was sold, but in actuality it meant a demotion as I would no longer be managing others. The course he suggested was a Master of Philosophy (MPhil) in Social Work. Although I had a qualification in Social Work, I did not hold a bachelor's degree because I had abandoned the degree in Psychology in preference for the social-work qualification. Academically speaking, it was a big leap to take. I wondered how on earth I could ever achieve this goal, and it seemed unattainable. It seemed like a poisoned chalice. I wondered if they wanted me to fail, but I decided that I would take the opportunity to learn.

My secondment was agreed, one day each week to complete a two-year course with fees being paid. I would keep my job until such time as I was ready to make the change. Consequently, I was being given the opportunity to study at a higher level for which I was ill-prepared. It seemed like a good deal but I could only think that I was being set up to fail. How would I do it? Where would the strength come from? It was the universal principle advocated by Hill and Stone (1987) that propelled me to believe that I could do it: 'What the mind of man can conceive and believe the mind of man can achieve'. (Hill and Stone, 1987).

Against my boss's insistence that there would be no reprieve of workload and his edict that I would fit five days' work into four, I accepted the challenge, was proactive and prepared myself for academic study. I armed myself with the following verse of Scripture:

> *Study to show thyself approved unto God, a workman that needeth not to be ashamed, rightly dividing the word of truth.*
>
> 2 TIMOTHY 2:15 (HOLY BIBLE)

Anything that is worth having is worth fighting for, even with the most stringent of requirements. The course was difficult but it was a new and ground-breaking experience for me that would in time take me towards my dream. As the course progressed, I appeared to be at a disadvantage.

I was required to study alongside a full-time job while other students were given the full support, space and time to study by their managers. The question of how I would gain the strength to complete this demanding course came as I had personal dialogue with my inner critic and created a picture in my mind of what success would look like if I could further develop the strength and tenacity that, according to my first manager, was already present within my personality. I would need to focus on self-denial, enthusiasm and perseverance. I spoke to my inner critic and defied the belief that I was incapable of achieving this level of study.

I turned to the Bible for a model of success and began to study the life of Jesus. I found that He was committed. He encouraged those who would follow Him to learn about self-denial and a life of dedication. He did not waver but constantly worked towards His calling. In short, He was proactive rather than reactive. Whether we profess to believe or not, these are principles that are timeless and work for our betterment. I adopted these principles and seamlessly integrated them into my thinking. I went to bed late and woke up early to get the coursework completed. I made every sacrifice imaginable to make possible what appeared to be impossible. The outcome of my intense dedication was the multi-layered success that followed.

The story that Hill and Stone told in their aforementioned book comes to mind. They wrote about a man who desired to find gold. He bought the equipment and went digging for this treasure. After some time, he became disillusioned and lost hope. He abandoned his search and returned the equipment to the shop. Days later another gold-digger bought the equipment and went in search of gold. He found the gold a short distance from where the man had given up his search. They said that often we do not realise that success comes to those who are willing to keep trying.

During the two years of study, I continued to work co-operatively with the team even though at times it was difficult. Nevertheless, I focused on becoming a critical thinker and was able to advise my supervisees on highly complex child-protection cases. I started to develop expertise and a sound knowledge base in my area of professional practice. I was no longer a rooky but a seasoned professional with the capacity to make decisions about the lives of vulnerable children in the welfare system. I had made a paradigmatic shift in my thinking.

As I neared the end of the course my patience and hard work paid dividends, because out of the ten students, only two completed and received the qualification, and I was one of them. It is a true saying that it is not where you come from but where you end up. Where I ended up had everything to do with my mind-set, my values, my way of thinking and my actions.

As I reflect on this time in my life, I can see that it was a process and a journey I had to go through. It was in going through this process that I was refined. It is only as we are tried as it were in fire that we are refined. This is how it is with gold when it emerges from the earth, it is not yet a fine quality product until it goes through the furnace and produces lasting value. A person in the Bible called Job had an experience of trial and tribulation. He concluded that it was only as he was tried that he was able to come forth as gold. Job 23:10 (HOLY BIBLE).

In the same way as my mother stood at the crossroads, so did I as I neared the end of my studies. Even though the circumstances differed vastly, it was a test of character and stamina. For me, it was as I was sitting at my desk that a call came through for me and answered the question: How would I achieve my dream? It came in the most unexpected way. The person on the other end of the line was the course director from the college where I had completed my qualification in Social Work. He remembered me because I had returned to the college on several occasions as a guest lecturer. The lesson I learnt that day is that it is more blessed to give than to receive. His words were precise. He said, 'Lynda we are looking for a lecturer to join our team. Would you be interested in applying?'. I could not believe that such an opportunity would come to me as I was nearing the end of my course and a decision would be made as to my next position. This call came at an opportune time and it provided another possibility that turned my life around. It is worth saying that it is the impression we leave on people's minds that causes them to remember us and, in many respects, brings success.

The question of how I would become successful came in the most unexpected way. As I sat waiting for the interview another candidate sat beside me. I was the first person to be called in for this interview. When I emerged from the room, the candidate whispered 'what did they ask you?'. In an unselfish way I told him some of the questions. However, it was my time, not his, and I was offered the job as a lecturer without reservation. Moreover, it was unbelievable that the venue where I would begin my teaching career was, at one time, the school where Miss Brown had humiliated me. I was to teach in the same room where I was taught, but with a different attitude towards learners.

I consulted with Mike, as was my custom when we had to make big decisions. I had a close and loving relationship with him and knew that he would listen and give me good advice. I told him that changing career would mean moving out of the management trajectory, and thus, it would mean taking a steep drop in salary. On the other hand, I would begin a new career with new possibilities. Mike held my hand up and bravely said, 'Go for it Mummy'. I took his advice and resigned from my post in readiness for stepping into a new role in an academic institution. It was a breakthrough to success.

It was the best decision I could have made at that time. As I was working out my notice it took boundless energy, plenty of faith and a lot of courage to write up my dissertation and submit it. The examiners had praise for the study but felt it needed a little more work. I gritted my teeth, refused to give up, and set to work. On the second submission I was granted an MPhil and graduated in the summer of 1996.

Lynda graduates with MPhil.

One of the things that happened while I was going through this course was that I was unaware of the possibility of transferring to the PhD programme. I believe that everything happens for a reason and that everything under the sun has a season. It was not my time to move onto more demanding and advanced academic study. Neither was it the time to take another financial risk. I concluded that my best option was to take one step at a time, familiarise myself with the new position and allow the status quo to continue since it was also a time when Mike was preparing to study to become a doctor. He started at medical school in 1991 and successfully completed his studies in 1998. I could repackage and reinvent myself while calling on the knowledge I had gathered over several years in practice and from my studies. There were possibilities on the horizon.

Becoming a Lecturer

> Go for the moon. If you don't get it, you'll still be heading for a
> star. Happiness lies not in the mere possession of money; it lies in
> the joy of achievement, in the thrill of creative effort.
>
> FRANKLIN D. ROOSEVELT.

During my first year of teaching, I noticed that many adult learners
came to their studies with a sense of fear and trepidation. They
doubted that they could make the grade. They lacked confidence and
some of them had low self-esteem. I knew the signs only too well. They
talked about their last encounter with formal education as when they
left school. Many of them had families and were mature students. They
questioned whether they could succeed. Some of the students came
with their personal issues and for them it was a time when they
wanted to create a new future and new possibilities. Some relationships with their partners ended as the students struggled to carve out a
new identity for themselves. There were ambitions I understood and
could identify with, arising out of my own experience. My first
response was to be empathetic showing that I could identify with
them, and help them to reach their goals.

When I stepped into the classroom it felt as if I was born for the job,
because I took to it like a fish takes to water. It felt as if it was my
calling, my habitat. It felt good to be following my passion and my
purpose. The students noticed my talent for teaching and I was given
tremendously positive feedback. One student said that she wished that
she could videotape me so that I could see myself. I was humbled by
this comment, but I continued to keep my feet firmly on the ground
and did not allow such comments to make me feel superior to other
lecturers on the team, but clearly, they too were aware of my skills. As
the mid- and end-of-term evaluations were received there was no
doubt about my capabilities. This was the beginning of a long and

145

successful career in teaching as I combined practice with theory and showed students the skill and benefit of knowledge transfer.

The passion I had was always noticed and commented on by students. When completing evaluations, they consistently commented on the enthusiasm and passion they saw in my eyes. Apparently, my eyes would light up. From my earliest days of lecturing a student told me that I had the gift of making the complex appear simple. I could easily blend theory with practice and make learning appear achievable. In this way they were given an invitation to learn as I demystified complex ideas making them reachable. These gracious comments came from the outset of my connections and interactions with learners and spanned a career that has lasted over twenty-six years. In the example below, a student sent a personal card of thanks and made this comment as he was leaving:

Dear Lynda, before I leave, I want to let you know that you are a fantastic teacher, your training has enhanced my social work skills. Thank you so very much. I have a lot of respect for you and hopefully you will continue contributing in this field. Thanks for your time, and energy.

It was during my first year of teaching that I sent the dissertation that I had completed for my MPhil to publishers and it was accepted as worthy of publication. The study I had completed was original and the first of its kind in the United Kingdom. It was exciting to make my mark in the field of research. My first publication was called *Making it Alone* and was published by the British Agencies for Adoption and Fostering (Ince 1998). As a result of this publication, I was invited to write a chapter in an edited text called 'The Reality of Research with Children and Young People.' (Lewis et al 2004)

Based on qualitative interviews with young black people preparing to leave the public care system, the study gave a bird's-eye view into their experiences. The lack of insight into their needs and the dereliction of duty on the part of local authorities had a negative impact on their lives during and after their leaving the public care system. They were placed trans-racially or in residential establishments. It was during this process that their identity was stripped away. They were not prepared as they made one of the most difficult transitions into adulthood because they knew very little about their heritage; they suffered from self-hate, and lacked the most basic of life skills. They were ill-prepared to enter the real world. It was an area of professional practice where I made my mark.

Separation, loss of family, culture and disconnection from the wider community were a key theme in this study. Their stories were a timely reminder of how my mother, as a single parent, had saved my siblings and me from this unwieldy system. The young people's experiences reinforced for me the importance of understanding the impact of separation and loss as well as the importance of family and identity. Many students and professionals have benefited from this study as they have learnt the importance of caring for children and preparing them for life. This was the point at which I became known as a keynote speaker and a guru on the topic of Preparing Young People for Transition to Adulthood. I wonder if you remember the boy who visited the unit where I worked who spoke in a derogatory way? This study was completed for children like him. It was a way of making a contribution to the learning of others.

As it happened, my position as Senior Lecturer placed me in the right environment to attend conferences, taking on the role as keynote speaker to educate others about the findings of my research. Moreover, it allowed me to move from my comfort zone and into the stretch zone. I quickly became known on the conference circuit and networked with universities and other organisations that invited me to train their staff in an area of social work that was fast captivating the minds of policy makers, and with organisations fighting for the rights of young people and how to prepare them for adulthood. The evidence provided from this study led to many opportunities to train qualified staff to work with vulnerable children because the findings could be extrapolated and applied to a wider group of young people.

Immediately after the publication of my book *Making it Alone*, I was successful in gaining an honorarium to attend a symposium to present the findings of my research at Florida State University. Money and the material things we gain are not a true measure of success, but the influence we exert has a greater part to play.

Eventually, I moved to the University of Hertfordshire and worked in a position as Senior Lecturer. I taught Childcare, Research Methods and Practice Teaching while supervising students in the field. I was now diversifying and my knowledge base was influencing others. It was at this stage that it became clear where my final destination would be. My aim was to be an educator, a mentor and a consultant. This feeling was intensified when I was studying for my master's and asked a person who had achieved this status for help. She bluntly told me: 'Go to the library'. I determined in my heart that day that if God allowed me to succeed at my studies, I would do all I could to help and mentor students. The desire to help others set the platform for my success.

While working at the University of Hertfordshire it was discovered that there were several lecturers who had not attained a master's or higher qualification. It became a requirement to gain a qualification in Higher Education, namely a master's, or a doctorate. I already had an MPhil, therefore I successfully completed the postgraduate course in teaching in higher education. As one millennium came to an end and the world was ushered into a new century, there was considerable fear gripping the nation and the world about what would happen. It was at this time of uncertainty that I registered at the University of Birmingham to complete my doctoral studies on a part-time basis while continuing to hold my post as Senior Lecturer at the University of Hertfordshire, England.

During my years of teaching, I consistently received contracts to work independently, thus I decided to reduce my teaching hours and set up a business as a Freelance Trainer and Consultant. By the third year of my studies, I made a decision to give up my job as a lecturer to concentrate on my business and my studies. It was a bold, audacious and risky step, but again I launched out in faith believing that I could do it. The authors Kathryn and Ross Petras (2014) in their book '*It always seems impossible until it's done* state in their introduction that, 'We need to be reassured that failing is not the end of the world, but possibly a wonderful beginning' (iii). Based on my personal knowledge and experience, I can attest to this statement.

I was ready to take on a new challenge. Starting a new business took time and a lot of willpower. I had to do it by faith, but with time and plenty of effort I reached the goals I had set out to achieve. I have heard it said that faith is an anchor on shifting sand. This statement is true because faith was my anchor during times of uncertainty. It was the key that unlocked many doors and helped me to engage with a positive mindset. My business became successful as I created my personal brand of courses and successfully provided consultancy and staff training within the social care and business sectors. The notion that I could achieve anything I set my mind to was an idea that my mother had planted in my mind, not necessarily by using the words, but by modelling it through her behaviour, quiet endeavours and actions. Most of my work came through recommendations.

There is a sense in which you begin a journey through a tunnel, but as time passes, you cannot see the light at the end of that tunnel, yet you cannot turn back. Therefore, the only solution is to move forward, keep pressing forward. There is no 'get out clause' so you have to move upward and onward. This was what happened to me as I was creating a new venture and was completing my doctorate. I felt as if I wanted to turn back, but I knew that turning back was not an option I could take. Consequently, it was the urge to finish my thesis that would not allow me to abandon it. The long hours of study meant that I was burning the candle at both ends. It was arguably one of the most rigorous and difficult projects I have ever undertaken. Yet, it was exciting and drove me to the edge of my own personal resources.

The allotted time for a part-time PhD is ten years. I was working mostly in isolation and with intermittent support from my advisors. By the time I reached the sixth year of study I was exhausted and at the deep end, but I continued until my back gave way. The university where I had chosen to complete my studies was a long journey from my home. On one occasion I was ready to set out on my journey at 6.00 a.m. As I bent down to pick up the newspaper, I heard something snap in my lower back. Nevertheless, I left home with the intention of meeting my appointment with my supervisors. By the time I reached Euston International Station in London, the pain was excruciating. I was wheeled onto the train but I could not sit. When I got on the train, I called Mike and he advised me to stand as much as I could. I made the journey there and back home. That is how determined I was to achieve my goal.

The stress was proving to be more than I could handle sensibly. I decided to take time out and slow down. The university agreed a six-month break after which I came back to my studies with renewed vigour and energy. The strength came from knowing that if I took small steps and applied the principle of producing some work each day it would, in the end, lead to tangible results. My intention was to grow out of my truth, based ostensibly on my experiences. One lesson I have learnt over the years, is that I was not entitled to anything unless I worked hard for it. It was only then that I could claim true victory.

God always sends someone to give a helping hand. He opens doors of opportunity even when we are not cognisant of it. My help during this time came from two study supervisors at the University of Birmingham, England, who appreciated the merit of the research I was completing. I sent them chapters and they read them and sent feedback. When the feedback came it often had red marks and my initial response was to become discouraged and despondent, but I learnt how to set it aside, returning to it when I was in a more positive frame of mind. One of the lessons I learnt throughout the long process of studying is that Rome truly was not built in a day. One has to position one block at a time; patience is the master art. I reached a stage where I was invited to present the initial findings of my research at Fresno State University, California, and later on at the University of Illinois, Chicago. Both were opportunities that opened doors for me to defend my thesis.

Family and friends are important sources of support. This was certainly the case with a few people who read the thesis and gave timely feedback. My sister, Gozil, had already gained her doctorate in nursing and was very supportive particularly as I was working on the research methodology. Each member of my family gave support in different ways, some of them too numerous to mention. I always took work on my holidays. I recall sitting at Los Angeles airport with my sister Pauline, and together we meticulously checked the bibliography. It was a labour of love. I identify with the words of Paul the Apostle when he said:

> Therefore, my beloved brethren, be ye steadfast, unmovable, always abounding in the work of the Lord. For as much as ye know that your labour is not in vain in the Lord.
>
> 1 CORINTHIANS 15:58 (HOLY BIBLE)

Sometimes people come into our lives for a reason. I cannot write about this type of support without mentioning my friend Ronny. I met her as I was standing at the copying machine at a university where I was a guest lecturer. She recognised me as the author of '*Making it Alone.*' Out of a short conversation, she became a constant friend during this period. Not only did she help by reading my thesis, but also, she gave me an opportunity to write distance-learning materials for The Open University where she was working. Life is strange because this was the university where I first began my learning journey.

As I approached the end of my thesis Ronny introduced me to a doctor who was lecturing at the University of Bristol and he became

151

instrumental in reading the final draft of my thesis. Feedback is worthwhile and critical to success because it causes one to pause, reflect and think. We often have the tendency to lack critical thinking particularly when it is about our own performance. We fear that another person's critical thinking might be judgemental. Jack Canfield (2015) makes the point that we tend to prefer positive feedback, but negative feedback 'tells us that we are off course' and he refers to negative feedback as 'improvement opportunities.' This is true because it was only as I took what I immediately internalised as negative feedback and turned it into critical feedback that the quality of my work improved and eventually brought success.

I began to visualise myself gaining an award, wearing the distinctive cap and gown. During the final stages of writing my thesis I took a trip to Barbados, the land of my descendants, and worked on the final corrections. This was where it all began. Against the hurdles and setbacks, I kept the picture of my graduation day firmly rooted in my mind and my consciousness, until I walked up a long corridor at one of the most prestigious universities and submitted my thesis to the Department of Social Policy. As I turned it over to the administrators, I walked back down the corridor with tears of joy in my eyes and a spring in my step. I held the vision of success until the day I entered a forbidding room and defended my thesis.

The questions came in quick succession and I answered them with precision and confidence. Mike and Joy were sitting outside and when I emerged from the examination room, I felt that I had not done well, but they supported and surrounded me with their love. One of the doctors who was present in the room followed me and she embraced me, saying 'you did such a good job'. Yet, in that moment, I refused to believe that I could have impressed others with my work. I was invited back into the room and the words were uttered, 'Well done Dr Ince'. I looked up to the ceiling and said 'Thank you God'. I felt as if I was allowed into a special club. It was a cause for great rejoicing, thanksgiving and jubilation. I had moved from failing at school, to becoming a single parent to becoming a leader to becoming a PhD. Most people would say what I achieved was impossible. I would say that with God all things are possible to those who believe. It was the end of a long journey that took nine years of hard work, stubborn determination, willpower and unquestionable motivation, yet I felt as if I was on the cusp of a new journey.

Personal Reflections

Lynda at her Graduation.

Success comes to us in different ways. One man's bread might very well be another man's poison. One size does not fit all, and we have different ways of achieving our objectives. I worked quietly but consistently to achieve the goals that would enable me to succeed. Albert Bandura a psychologist said:

> In order to succeed, people need a sense of self-efficacy, to struggle together with resilience to meet the inevitable obstacles and inequalities of life.

> ALBERT BANDURA (1997)

For me, the key to defining success is an inner feeling of joy, happiness, satisfaction, and knowing that I have done my best. From the most menial to the most demanding task, I try to do my best. Achieving and reaching a goal requires sacrifice and dedication, which is a true mark of success. The desire that burns within a person for success should be far greater than the fear of failure.

Material possessions that most people try to acquire are good and desirable. They ultimately come from our endeavours but we cannot look to our possessions as the only way of defining the meaning of success or the only way of ultimately finding happiness and contentment. On the other hand, we should not think that we are incapable of attaining or attracting the best things in life. Remember that the cattle on a thousand hills belong to God and the scriptures say that it is His good pleasure to give us the kingdom. This means that there is nothing we cannot achieve if our hearts and motives are in the right place.

To be successful there are principles and ethical values we must apply with unfailing regularity. These principles and values are alluded to in many of the books that deal with success, as well as in personal stories from those who have made it to the pinnacle of their careers or of any endeavour in which they engage. The principles I have applied are sacrifice, hard work, motivation, consistency, determination, discipline, balance and creativity. Such principles may not all be applied at the same time, but depending on an individual's circumstance, they will discover the combination that is best fitted to the success they are seeking.

Success is all about taking opportunities as they come. In order to take an opportunity, we must be aware of its presence. There are times when we actively look for opportunities and they may or may not materialise. When an opportunity does not match up to our expectations it is important to hold onto whatever dream we have formulated in our minds and to carry it around looking for the next opportunity to fulfil it.

Throughout this chapter I have outlined the various ways that opportunities came to me. Some of them involved taking risks, some involved thinking about change, some involved being proactive, some involved waiting, and some required patience and endurance. Some came when I least expected, and some came when I was at a point where I desired to turn my life around. Opportunities always materialised as I took action.

In my work as a life coach, I talk to people about the importance of goal-setting and being action-oriented. I demonstrate how I reached my goals and I give clients and course participants life examples and self-directed activities that are meaningful to them. As I work with groups, I encourage participants to share their experiences. It is a way of giving back and enriching the lives of others through meaningful communication and sharing of ideas.

I have found that success came when I moved out of my comfort zone, moved into the stretch zone and took sensible risks. This is when I experienced the most growth. I realise that growing is a staged process; it takes time to become successful. If success comes overnight, it is hardly worth it, because there will be no track record of what we did to achieve, and nothing to share with others that will help them to grow.

There will be no legacy to leave behind. The things we achieve in this life almost always come on the back of failure, sacrifice and hard work, and when we are declining in hope and inspiration. It is at this time that going the second mile makes the difference. Success is not meteoric because we must be able to look back and assess growth by stages. For me, all human progress is built on stages. It does not come if we engage in self-limiting beliefs; if it did, it would not be highly prized and appreciated.

CHAPTER ELEVEN

Gains and Losses

Life is not linear, therefore there are peaks and troughs in our everyday lives. It was during the period of my studies that I experienced two significant and painful losses. The first was my mother. At that time, she was living with me. I continued to work and at the same time carried out my field research while becoming a carer for her. As I transcribed the data, I read the *verbatim* stories of the participants to Mama. She listened intently and then expressed sadness for the children whose lives were filled with loss, anguish, hopelessness, powerlessness and bitterness. She passed away before I could finish my doctorate, but not before she had given me the courage to keep striving for my goal. Her death had a significant impact on me, but I was grateful for the positive memories and the many lessons she taught me. She knew when it was her time to go and she passed away peacefully and without a struggle at the age of eighty-five years.

Mama had a successful life not in terms of riches, but in terms of blessings, an unusual brand of knowledge and insight. She always had some unique Barbadian expressions that had deep significance and meaning that always made her children laugh. They were stored in her head, never written down anywhere. They were a treasure trove of knowledge gained from life that she effortlessly passed onto her children. This was the essence of her wisdom and character.

Her study of the Bible enabled her to encourage others and guide them with a good level of proficiency. She had raised eight children and left an unbelievable legacy of love and words of wisdom that we will always remember and cherish. To our family she was a matriarch and a good role model, to her church members she was a leader, in her community she was a contributor, to her friends she was a helper and to her children's offspring she was a loving grandmother and to children, without blood ties, she was a mother in Israel.

These are the successes she realised through her children; these were the gains:

Of the nine children Mama gave birth to, one died at the age of six. The eldest, Grace, became a nurse and was successful in her career. Judy was a typist and did clerical work until she retired. Gozil was a trailblazer; she was the first member of our family to immigrate to the United States. She qualified as a nurse in the UK and completed her midwifery training. She gained her master's while living in New York and her doctorate in nursing from the University of California, San Francisco, in 1994. After completing her doctorate, she taught at Fresno State University, and was promoted to Professor in 1999. When she retired in 2008, she was awarded the prestigious title of Professor Emerita in Nursing. Pauline trained as a secretary and went on to work for directors and did well within her chosen field. She gained her degree in Business Studies and has written two books of poetry. Denise qualified as a barrister at Gray's Inn London and completed her pupillage at the Chambers of Leonard Woodley QC, Temple. She is an active member of Lincoln's Inn. She relocated to San Diego and took the equivalent examinations, which allowed her to set up her own business and practise Family Law. Daryl, my only brother, gained his degree at Oxford Polytechnic and became a civil engineer and worked for English Heritage. Joy trained as a fashion designer at the London College of Fashion. She relocated first to New York and then to Michigan where she completed a BBA in Accounting degree at Andrews University. Joy currently lives in Philadelphia and works for the United States Federal Government. She also trains and coaches newly hired government employees.

My personal successes are documented in this book and are a tribute to my mother. Although her desire to become a teacher did not materialise, her children achieved many successes of which she could be proud. She did not miss a celebration or a graduation. She was also the proud grandmother of seven grandchildren and one great granddaughter.

I do not mind repeating that it is true that it is not where you begin that matters, but rather where you end up. Yet, when I look back at my life, I would conclude that I was not destined to end up where I did. The idea of pulling oneself up by the boot laces has merit that many people would do well to learn. This saying was proven on several occasions, but more so on a day in 1994 when my son passed his medical examinations. This opened the door to greater successes as he worked hard, applied himself and persevered until he became a General Practitioner and then a Senior Partner at the surgery where he has established his career. At the time of writing my memoir, he is the Director of the Medical Federation which is seeking to drive change and better access for patients in the locality where he works. He is well respected by professionals and patients. He has been blessed with a

beautiful son called Lenny, giving me the desire of my heart to be a proud grandmother.

Becoming a grandmother is one of life's marvels and a tremendous gain for me. There is an undeniable connection between the role of being a mother and a grandmother. For me becoming a mother was a gift but becoming a grandmother was the extra bit of icing on the cake. It gave me a feeling of being blessed to see another generation in my family. My sister, Denise, told me that raising my son was my real job, parenting him was a labour of love and my true calling. Having a grandchild is not a job, but it requires some of the qualities of parenting but without the

Lenny wins gold medal 50 metres breast stroke

ultimate responsibility. I conceived of this role as an extraordinary blessing the day I first held my grandson in my arms. As I sat at East Surrey hospital where he was born, I did not want to let him go. Becoming a grandmother gave me the opportunity to enjoy spending time with this very special little person who has come into my life. My only regret is that my mother and brother passed away before my grandson was born.

The Cancer Journey

My brother was born during a hurricane. It was called Hurricane Janet. My mother arrived home with him as the entire community was being evacuated to a nearby school for shelter from the impending doom. From the day my father died he was destined to become the male figure that we would look to for support. Without knowing it he was placed in the father-figure role and carried a tremendous burden for his sisters. I recall that one day I was at work and received a call from the carer to say that Mama had fallen. I rushed home, and when I arrived Daryl was there taking care of her needs. I was anxious but he calmly said, 'Lynda leave it to me.' In these modern times it is unusual for boys to remain at home past the age of eighteen, but my brother lived at home until his later 20s, and until he decided that he wanted to complete a degree in Civil Engineering. He visited us regularly and did not ever forget the anniversary of Daddy's death.

The cancer journey began long before we knew about it. Stress had taken its toll on him. He felt a real sense of responsibility for each one of his sisters and his mother. He could be relied upon and we called on him frequently for advice and practical support. Without another male figure in our family, it was easy to become over-reliant on him. The demands of his family, work and interest in golf kept him busy.

In the midst of life, and when we least think it possible, we are in the midst of death. It was just four years after my mother had passed away that I also lost my only brother. It was a significant loss that came at a time when my business was beginning to take off and I was working hard on my research. My brother went to California to support my sister. She was recovering from a brain haemorrhagic stroke. He came back looking gaunt and in considerable pain in his stomach. He began to question if it could be that he had the same complaint as our dad. We brushed these thoughts aside, because we thought that life could not be that cruel. He told me that one day he was at work and the pain stunned him to the ground. It was then that we began to search for our dad's death certificate and discovered that our father had died from pancreatic cancer. His condition was exactly the same as our father, the only difference was that he was given the timing of his death. The demon Cancer had returned like a destroying angel to haunt my family and take our brother. It was an unbelievable twist of fate. Herein was the next devastating loss that brought back memories of my father.

The cancer journey began the day when I, along with his partner Julie, sat in the oncology department of the hospital where he was waiting to hear the results of his test and with it the hope that they could fit a stent to alleviate his pain. We were sitting in the waiting area for what seemed like hours. For the second time in my life a surgeon walked into the room with bad news. The news was that Daryl was in the last stages of pancreatic cancer, with the pronouncement that the cancer had spread to his liver, making it impossible to perform an operation. The oncologist gave him six months to live. This level of disbelief was like a mortal blow and was unpalatable. My sense of disbelief caused me to ask if there was anything he could do to change this diagnosis. I could not contain my emotions and rushed to the ladies' toilet where I broke down and cried uncontrollably. When I had regained my composure, I walked back into the room, hoping for different news, but there was none. I found Daryl deciding who would inherit his golf clubs. The look of despair on his face was one that I will never forget.

As fate would have it, I had an appointment to interview a couple that evening that was in the direction towards my home. I decided to stop and let them know that I could no longer carry on due to the emotional state that had taken a grip on me. When I arrived at my destination, I found myself incapable of holding onto my grief and almost fell at their door. These strangers allowed me to sit in their home and comforted me until I could undertake the journey home. The journey took me half an hour, but it was the longest half an hour I had ever driven. In an attempt to ease my pain, I randomly placed a CD in the player and the song I heard was by Don Moen. It was called 'God will make a way'.

As I drove down the dark, lonely and winding road towards home, all I could think about was how I would ever get over not having my brother around. Thus, I hoped against hope that the oncologist had made a mistake, and If he had, he would surely be forgiven. As I think about that day, my keenest sense was hearing. I heard the words of the surgeon ringing and reverberating in my ears amongst the tears, and there was a sense of confusion and dismay.

There were days when I found it difficult to find the words to express my thoughts. At these times, I used my journal to express my deep feelings of overwhelming emotions. However, when the pain became intolerable, I simply abandoned the journal, but I always returned to it. Today my journaling gives a full account of what happened as I went through this roller coaster journey, as well as how I recovered.

This brief excerpt from my journal indicates the level of emotional pain I was experiencing throughout this distressing journey:

We went to see Daryl at Mount Vernon Hospital today and spent the entire afternoon with him. Today he told us of a sharp pain in his legs. He said that the pain was so severe that he felt as if someone had stabbed him, and he looked to see if his leg was bleeding. The worst thing about this disease is the pain and suffering it causes, as well as the speed with which it is progressing. It is so debilitating. It is so sad to see Daryl go through so much pain, that I am in tears every day. On three occasions I narrowly missed accidents on the road. I am finding it hard to concentrate. The tears just flow. Sometimes I think that Daryl is strong and other times I think that he is afraid. These are feelings, but I too fear these feelings. This roller-coaster journey has taken us all by storm. Daryl was born in a storm and he is dying in a storm. We say the Lord's Prayer and the 23rd Psalm with him to give him courage. It must be so hard for him.

There were many things I recorded during his illness. I recall that in the early stages of his illness, I had a meeting some distance from my home, and he offered to drive me to the location. As we travelled, he talked about many things and we enjoyed our time together. The other was a memorable weekend we spent together. As we travelled by car to our destination, he asked me a pertinent question that allowed me to go through the process of grieving and at the same time complete my studies. The question was simple, what is your thesis about? Without hesitation I spoke with confidence to him about the findings of my research as if I was defending it. Knowing that his days were numbered, he encouraged me to complete the work and get it out into the community to benefit others. His admiration for what I was trying to achieve injected a huge amount of confidence into my soul.

Being Fearless

Henry David Thoreau, a poet and philosopher, put the case well when he said a person should live the life they have always dreamt of, be fearless in the face of adversity and recognise the beauty around them. This statement sums up what I feel about my brother. I remember my brother as a person with audacious dreams. He had high ideals, he was fearless when he met with obstacles and he saw the beauty that was around him. He loved children and was a mentor to my son as he was growing up; in fact, they had a father-son relationship that allowed him to manoeuvre Mike though his adolescence. He became an avid cricketer, and a golfer at a time when black men were not accepted in this up-market, middle-class and costly sport. He had lofty and grandiose dreams and was not afraid to test out his ideas.

His interest in the advancement of young people led him to become the founding member of a golf club called 'Eagles'. His intention was to give youngsters an opportunity to have a bite of the cherry. He was enthusiastic; full of energy, he had buckets of zest for life, and his laughter would light up any room. He wanted to share his talent for golf with young people. He won many trophies, some of which he did not tell us about. We only discovered the extent of his talent when he died. In the photograph my brother stands proudly

Daryl and Mike.

with one of his trophies shaking my son's hand.

As plans were being made to transition him to a hospice, sadly, we knew that his end was near. Another twist of fate was that he died on February 14th 2007 (Valentine's Day). It was one day before my husband had passed away thirty-six years earlier. February is a hugely significant month for me because my father, mother, son and I were all born in that month. My husband and my brother died during that month. During the time my brother had to live he said, 'who would have thought that I would be the next to go?'. What made his loss deep was that he was the first of the siblings to die and he was the only male sibling.

Shortly after his death, I was travelling on a train and sitting opposite to me was a man drinking alcohol out of a bottle at 8.30 a.m. He was dishevelled and beaten up by his habit. I was filled with anger and asked God how it could be that this man was being allowed to live when my brother with all his life ahead of him and all of his potential had to die. I complained inwardly about the fact that I did not feel this was just or fair. When I realised what I was doing, I asked God to forgive me for thinking in this way. I remembered that we have no say in who should live and who should die. Yet, it was my close attachment with and love for my brother that contributed to this feeling. It was a rude awakening for me.

I have learnt many lessons from life and one of them is that we cannot choose when or how we die unless we make the decision to end our lives before the appointed time. When my brother was given the diagnosis, it felt like the end of the end. It felt as if an important part of my family unit was being taken away without warning. It was a replica of my childhood experience of death and its devastating effect on my life.

During the six months that were given to him we made the most of it. The hardest part of this journey was watching him fade away and feeling a sense of hopelessness and helplessness. Part of the journey was holding on, giving encouragement when I felt less encouraged and holding onto the belief that one day according to God's promise, I would see him again.

Personal Reflections

Losing my mother and my brother were significant losses because they meant so much to me. Both had made a great impression on my mind and were my anchors. Although my mother's death was expected, it was a bitter blow because she was the person who gave me hope and she helped me to enlarge my territory. Losing my brother was also psychologically crippling because of the role he played in my family. He was dependable. We worked on many projects together, including building a granny flat to my home so that Mama could live with me during the last stages of her life.

Daryl's loss was a difficult experience because his death came in quick succession to the loss of our mother and when we were just beginning to accept that she had gone from us. I remember him as a person with high standards and unquestionable loyalty and commitment to his family. He had a way of protecting his sisters that made him a very important person in my eyes.

The loss of my mother and brother were different from the loss of my husband because in both instances I had time to say goodbye. We used the time to share past memories and to talk about times gone by. At times my experience was filled with anguish, pain and sadness, but knowing that my mother had lived a long and productive life gave me the opportunity to look back on her life with optimism. Her belief that death was not the end enabled me to eventually come to terms with this loss knowing that death is but a sleep.

In my brother's case I was able to sit by his bedside, we brought photographs and other memorabilia, and as a family we reminisced about the good times. When we searched for answers as to why he should die there were no answers. Daryl was brave and made preparation in his final hours. As a family we told him that we loved him and would miss him. We told him that we would be by his side until the end. I was able to weep with him, laugh with him and sigh with him. I was given the opportunity to help and support him through this time of crisis. It was the act of going through this process, being able to hold his hand, to sit by his bedside, express emotions, say words of love, show appreciation, and be present as he took his last breath that, with time, I was able to let go. It was a process that brought closure and healing, but not the ability to forget the positive and enduring impact my brother had on my life. The legacy we leave behind is the difference we have made to the lives of others. I will always remember my brother for his sincerity and devotion to others.

Life could never be quite the same again because two of the bright lights and strongest leaders in my close-knit family had gone, but they have left a legacy that we are holding onto. I noticed that as siblings, we all had different reactions to grief even though we had experienced the same loss. The one common factor between us was the different stages of grief, timing and acceptance. In order to go through the process of grieving without disintegrating, we had to maintain contact with each other even though some of my sisters were living in the USA and even though it was difficult to talk. The difference between us was the ease or lack of ease with which we were able to talk about our feelings of grief, sadness and loss. I recall that one day as I was writing my journal about my brother and the cancer journey I broke down and cried. I immediately called Denise and she comforted me. We talked about the good times and what our brother meant to us. I discovered that we had different experiences and could draw on them to make a composite picture of his life. In this way we were able to see the bigger picture. Althea Pearson (1994) talks about a concept called 'reframing'. It is a therapeutic response to loss that requires creating a picture in a person's mind that turns a negative into a positive. To my way of thinking, as we spoke, we turned around my negative emotion created by feelings of loss and helplessness into a positive discourse. Thus, turning around negative events is a healing process that was part of my recovery.

With loss there are also gains. Although Mama and Daryl passed away, I was granted the joy of having a grandson. One does not replace one with the other, but I am grateful that joy came after pain and that ashes turned into beauty.

It was after the death of my mother and brother that I began to think about the next contribution I could make to the lives of others. As I was reaching retirement years, I could not see myself sitting at home spending endless hours watching the television or gazing at the ceiling. As I was thinking of the next direction, I had a call from my niece. History repeats itself in miraculous ways. As I told her that I was thinking about what I could do as a bridge to retirement, she said, 'Aunty Lynda, you have so many skills in working with people. You could become a Life Coach'. I immediately looked online for a course in Performance Life Coaching. Having found it, I completed the course and gained a Diploma. During the sessions I had wonderful feedback from the tutors and my fellow students. The encouragement I received allowed me to know that I could become an authentic life coach.

Lynda's energy draws you in, lovely style. It was when she talked about the lenses through which we see the world and the messages and how she was drawn to become a life coach that impressed me. She is very knowledgeable. Thank you, Lynda

The tutor's comments at the end of the course were enlightening because she acknowledged and celebrated the work I had done.

I love the depth that explained all the coaching behaviours and your detailed reflections of your learning throughout the course is superb. Your dedication to learning and development during this course has been awesome and on top of the course work you came up with the six E's model which showed your philosophy of coaching. Well done, Lynda.

It was her comment about my detailed reflections and my dedication to learning that confirmed the principles I had been committed to from the day I began my teaching career. I became excited at moving into this new direction where I could help others to set goals and hold steadfastly to them.

Working with people on a one-to-one basis or in groups allows them to search for answers through a process of reflection, visualisation and affirmation. As the answers to their concerns and worries emerge, they are energised to think in new ways. They are able to set out action plans, to visualise their dreams, to face fear and take a chance, in order to get to where they want to be. I have been fortunate to coach many people; they all come with different needs and desires, but all of them were dissatisfied with some aspect of their lives and wanted to make changes. I have been successful in delivering workshops on the principles that lead to success for leaders and have been amazed by the feedback and affirmation I have received.

As we let our own lights shine, we unconsciously give other people the permission to do the same. As we are liberated from our own fears our presence automatically liberates others.

NELSON MANDELA, PEACE PRIZE WINNER 1993

CHAPTER TWELVE

A Second Chance

Difficulties are opportunities to better things; they are stepping stones to greater experiences ... when one door closes, another always opens, as a natural law it has to be, to balance.

BRYAN ADAMS

Have you ever driven by a particular area and did not see something that was there all along? But for some reason you passed by and just did not see it. Then one day and for no particular reason you suddenly noticed it. Nothing had changed, the landscape was the same, it was there but you did not see it or you were not meant to see it. That is what happened to me. Have you been waiting for something good to happen but it seemed that the door was closed and you could not get past it? That is what happened to me.

I had been living my life on a busy thoroughfare and had achieved more than I ever felt was possible in my lifetime. I was able to reach many of my goals, to travel to many destinations and see how people live their lives. I had time to study and was successful in developing others and myself. I had managed to turn my life around.

Outwardly, I showed all the signs of being contented with my life but something was missing. I did not have a companion to share my life with. I began to pray silently asking God to provide me with a companion. On this issue He seemed to be silent. I had a limited social life and, in some respects, I was living an unbalanced life. Every activity I engaged in was work, church or study-focused. Most people in the circles I interacted with were married or had a partner, and those who were not married did not express an attraction for me or vice versa. I could not understand how it was possible to meet so many people in the course of my work, be told that I was an inspirational and authentic person and not meet someone who desired to be with me in a romantic way. This seemed paradoxical.

To a greater extent there was safety within the circles I inhabited. I felt that this was not a path I would have naturally chosen, but by some design it was created for me. Feeling safe was one thing, but feeling lonely was another. The hard truth was that I felt as if I would never meet a soul mate so I closed the door and made the best of my life. It was after Mike left home that I first felt the need for a companion, but I resisted getting involved with anyone because I also loved my independence, my work and my freedom.

The problem with maintaining a closed-life attitude was how it reduced possibilities, but I accepted this as the status quo because it felt safe. I told myself that once I came home, there was no one to tell me what to do, there were no expectations, no misunderstandings, no upsets, no having to say I am sorry and certainly nothing to make me worried or afraid. I had lived in the same house for over forty years; I knew my neighbours and had a good relationship with them. I was well established and to some extent contented with my life. I made the choices that suited me. I had no responsibility for or to any other human being except for the commitment I had to my son, my extended family, colleagues, friends and those I interacted with on a regular basis through my work connections. I had created and could maintain my own brand of independence and I was content with it. The problem was that I allowed life to drift along like a ship without a sail. I did not have the courage to step out in faith in this area of my life. I believed the traditional message I heard which was that a woman should not make the first move in finding a partner. It was better, according to the proverbial saying, to play hard to get. Yet, if I did not leave the shore behind, it would be impossible to have a second chance and a new experience. I would have held on to the past, failing to see new possibilities.

I grew up with the work ethic, hence work automatically replaced the need in me to find satisfaction in another person. I lived out my passion and my life purpose because my life was bound up in a career of service. My endless studies took over my life and kept me going. Home and work-life rolled into one, with no clear division between these two things. In essence, work became my main driver. I contented myself with this state of affairs. I convinced myself that it was better to be alone and happy, than being with another person and feeling unhappy. The question in my mind was whether I was truly happy and what constituted happiness. Was my perception of happiness what I had experienced before? Was it something I had been robbed of and would never regain? Was it something I had come to accept? I asked myself, was it possible to be given a second chance? I had no real answers. My predicament was in every sense of the word a conundrum.

If you want your life to change you must take action and alter the way you perceive the world around you. After forty-seven years of being in a perpetual state of widowhood I launched out into the deep. I did what I was coaching others to do. I took an action step and I took it in faith, not knowing what the outcome would be or even if my actions would produce a good outcome or one that I could live with and accept. I just knew that it was time to do something to turn things around. Sitting and hoping and wishing would not create the change I wanted and needed.

It was at this stage of my life that I yearned to be settled and happy and I wanted to maintain the idea of being courageous. It was Eleanor Roosevelt who said:

> You gain strength, courage and confidence by every experience in which you really stop to look fear in the face. You must do the thing that you think cannot be done.
>
> (ELEANOR ROOSEVELT)

Gaining Courage

There are many verses in the Bible that speak about courage. Each day we face situations that call for courage, whether it is in our personal lives, in our families or in our work life. Each day there is a battle to be fought and a battle to be won.

During 2017 I suddenly had an attack of sciatica resulting from a protruding disc in my lower back. It was a resurgence of my earlier back-pain issues. The physical pain was at times more than I could bear. I was laid low for several months and could barely walk. I literally cried out to God for help and for healing. The desire to fight back once again became a strong theme in my recovery. In my consciousness was the fact that I was alone. I once again began to pray that God would provide the right person for me. As I was beginning to regain my strength Joy visited me to offer practical support. It was during this time that she expressed a desire to visit a church in London to hear a preacher she liked. Truthfully, I did not want to go, but with persuasion I decided to join her.

I visited this church for a second time and on a day when I felt least inclined to do so. As I approached the door I was welcomed with a bulletin. At the end of the day, it was my intention to leave it on the chair, but I was prompted by an inner spirit to place it in my handbag. I did not read the notices as I felt that they were not intended for non-members.

I had been praying with my sisters for two years via conference calling as we felt the need to enter into joint prayer sessions. This activity was motivated by our desire to invite God's healing and intervention in various aspects of our lives. It was on one of these occasions that I was reminded of a topic that was coincidentally covered in what the pastor had spoken about. In an effort to tell my sisters about the topic, I went to the wastepaper basket where I had discarded the bulletin the previous day and retrieved it. Consider that the bulletin was in my handbag for over two weeks before I decided to throw it away. I can only conclude that it remained in my handbag for a reason to be revealed at a later time.

It was only when I took time to read the reverse side that I saw an invitation to register to attend a banquet for widows and widowers. Could this be the chance I was waiting for? Although I did not know what the outcome would be, I reasoned that if I did nothing, any

possibility of moving out of my comfort zone would be lost. I had been in my comfort zone for too long, I needed to step out and grasp this opportunity. I reasoned that there was nothing to lose. Against my best judgement, mostly to do with fear, I gained the courage to register my wish to attend the banquet. The person on the other end of the phone said that it was late, but she agreed to place my name on the list as I fitted the criteria. On the day of the event, I spent several hours thinking and planning how I wanted to look and present myself. I wanted to look attractive.

As I entered the room, I sat close to the door. I felt a little intimidated, but I suddenly saw two ladies sitting together and I asked if I could join them. The position in which we were sitting was uncomfortable as there was a breeze wafting through an opening in a nearby door. One of them suggested that we should move to an alternative seating area. As we communicated and exchanged pleasant conversation, a man known to the ladies approached our table and introduced himself as Hubert with those famous words 'who is this beautiful lady?'. I laughed as I introduced myself. He drew up a chair, the conversation flowed effortlessly between us and the ladies were on the periphery. Hubert came across as an outgoing, vivacious person. I was strangely drawn to him. He disclosed that his wife had died seven years previously, but he spoke about her with compassion. I admired his boldness and his transparency. Hubert revealed that he did not attend the banquet with preconceived ideas, but like myself, he was praying for a partner. He had registered his intention to attend the banquet before he left England for a holiday in Montserrat.

Connections are very important because they bind people together in ways that they do not always understand or expect. Connections are invisible and we may not always know what is going on behind the scenes. Yet, within the universe plans are being made. God always has a plan. As my new acquaintance indicated that he had already chosen an adjacent table I joined him. We did not mingle but continued talking and laughing. It appeared as if we had known each other for a lifetime. The guest performer was a comedian and he was just what we needed to keep the conversation light-hearted and laughing. I love to laugh; it has always been a trait in my personality and a valuable tool. It was incredible to talk in a way that immediately connected us.

During our conversation the topic of family arose. As we did so I learnt that he knew one of my sisters. She attended the same church where he had been a member from his youth and he was acquainted with her. He asked questions to establish her identity. As he described the person he knew, it became clear that it was my sister, Judy. She had invited him to video-record the wedding of another of my sisters in 1987. He recalled the church where the wedding ceremony had been conducted, the name of the pastor

The day I met Hubert.

who officiated at the wedding and the location of the venue where the reception was held. The event was so clear in his mind that I admitted that these details could only belong to my family. We sat in awe of this connection. What was even more amazing was that he recalled visiting a home after the reception where he continued to video the party. Hubert quickly said, 'I still have the video in my attic'. Several months later when he retrieved the video, it was astounding to see that he had recorded the wedding, the reception and a party at my home. He had interviewed Mike and me, along with several other guests. His video was a historic relic of our time. Hubert did not really see me, and I did not see him in this chance meeting, even though we were both single at the time. He was later married and had two children from this relationship. I had remained a widow. He had crossed my path but I did not notice him. By the time of our second encounter, his wife had died from breast cancer, thus changing his status to the same as mine.

Rethinking that I had met Hubert in 1987 I had no conception that this chance meeting would come back like a revolving door through which I would enter under different circumstances. It was nothing short of a miracle when he revealed this story to me and produced the video as evidence. The God I thought had not listened to my prayer was saying 'I have someone in store for you, but you must be patient'. God's timing is different from our timing and His ways are different from our ways and far beyond our knowing.

> For my thoughts are not your thoughts, neither are your ways my ways, saith the Lord. For as the heavens are higher than the earth, so are my ways higher than your ways, and my thoughts than your thoughts.
>
> Isaiah 55:8-9 (Holy Bible)

At the end of the evening, he asked how I intended to return home. It was getting late, but nevertheless I told him that I had a return ticket for the train. I flippantly said, 'the same way I came'. In that instant he offered to drive me home. As we were travelling, he told me that he wanted to retire and return to Montserrat, his country of origin. My heart sank. As wisdom is the better part of valour, I kept quiet. He communicated with me during the week that followed and told me that he was attending a wedding the next weekend, but asked if he could see me again. At the wedding, he met a woman who appeared to like him. She immediately began to send him text messages, but he told her that he had met me and wanted to pursue a relationship with me. It was at that point that his commitment was tested, not in terms of words, but in action.

Proposal of Marriage

> There is no fear in love; but perfect love casteth out fear; because fear hath torment. He that feareth is not made perfect in love.
>
> I JOHN 4:18 (HOLY BIBLE)

The power of love is inestimable, it can happen at first sight or it can happen as a relationship develops over time. It was approaching one year since I had met Hubert when his proposal of marriage came. He told me that he was committed to me and wanted to spend the remainder of his life with me. After having experienced many disappointments, I had developed a distrust of men, I had been let down and it made me afraid to open myself up to another person. It was always the fear that held me back. When Hubert told me that he was committed to me, it immediately struck a chord, because in all the years of my 'loneliness' and yearning for a soul mate, no one had ever used that word to me. After what seemed like a lifetime of waiting, these were the words that made the connection for me. I decided to give my affirmation and accepted his proposal of marriage.

There were several factors I considered and each gave me the confidence to marry him. The first was that we were of the same faith. He was a committed Christian; therefore, I felt that I would not need to convince him of what my faith meant to me.

The second was that his track record of a happy marriage relationship demonstrated his commitment. As I was introduced to his friends and his colleagues, they showed high regard for him and each one spoke of his integrity and his capacity to care for others. On one occasion he invited me to join him for an end-of-year Christmas party hosted by his employer. Without hesitation a gentleman approached us and said that he would like his relationship with his wife to be like ours. What he saw was love and at our stage of life, he felt that we demonstrated a good example of a loving relationship. These types of comments came from people wherever we went.

An even more important factor for me was whether my son, my grandson and my siblings would connect with him. As he met or spoke to my family each one expressed happiness for us. Without hesitation, my son said, 'If you are happy, then I am happy'. His statement gave me confidence to follow the path I had chosen, knowing that Hubert was accepted. My grandson immediately struck up a relationship with him. He knew how to speak to children and it was very important to know that my grandson would feel comfortable around him. Lenny was seven years old when they met. When I told him that we were going to be married, he wanted to see my engagement ring and he was genuinely happy for us. His only fear appeared to be if he could still visit and have his room. With reassurance he settled down and accepted Hubert. In a similar way, his family and church friends accepted me and were happy for us. I immediately increased my family and circle of friends.

Planning Our Special Day

Unlike many brides today who invest in a wedding planner, I chose not to have one, but I enlisted the support of my sisters and we worked together as a team to make it a reality within seven months. Not only is a wedding a special day but the planning for it can be stressful and agonising. My thoughts were constantly fixed on each element down to the most minuscule details.

Working together is a tradition in my family and it was no less important as we planned our wedding. It was amazing how the tasks were simplified as each aspect fell into place to make it a successful and memorable day. We carefully made decisions about my dress, accessories, bridesmaids' dresses, the colour scheme, venue, flowers, the speaker, the reception, the photographer and our honeymoon. Each aspect of our wedding flowed in perfect symmetry on the day. The most amazing of all the arrangements was that I found the perfect wedding dress in the first shop I walked into. It was made just for me. It was quite amazing.

Hubert and I were married on September 30th 2018. It was a day of joy, jubilation and gladness. We stood in the same church where my sister Denise had been married thirty years previously. As I walked into the church, I heard the cheers, I saw my son and grandson at the door waiting for me. I heard the words 'you look stunning'. My son took on the role of 'father of the bride' and gave me away. I stood beside the man who would presently become my husband, ending years of singleness and solitude. It was a day far beyond my imaginings, hopes and dreams. We made our vows in the presence of God and more than one hundred guests.

Hubert had woken up that day with a sore throat and his voice was husky as he said, 'I do'. There was nothing that could keep him from making this commitment in the presence of our family and friends, some of whom had travelled across the Atlantic to be present for this moment. The day was filled with laughter and fun, warmth and good wishes. It was perfect in every way. At last, my dream of a second chance had become a reality.

Lynda and Hubert.

On our wedding day, September 30th 2018.

Lynda and Mike.

Lynda with her sisters Gozil, Judy, Pauline, Denise and Joy.

Personal Reflections

Second chances may or may not come, but the truth is that we need to be tuned-in to recognise chances as they come along, sometimes out of the clear blue. The story of a man who was hanging from the branch of a tree waiting to be rescued is a good example. He wanted to be saved, but the conflict was that he was too afraid to let go of the branch. Those who came to save him, asked him to let go, but his refusal to let go of the branch and take the chance meant that they all eventually left him and he died clinging to the one thing that could not save him.

A second chance can come after failure or disappointment; it can come after rejection, after illness, divorce, or the loss of a job. It can come after a stressful or traumatic event as it did in my case. It can come when we are at our lowest ebb, when we feel lonely, deserted, hopeless or even when we feel depressed and in despair, or when we have lost the will to carry on. Second chances come as we search diligently for them and as we engage with change. Others may think that we are undeserving of the first chance let alone a second chance, but we should not allow how people feel to determine our outcome. What really matters is what you think of yourself and the equivalent effort that you are willing to put in to make the second chance a reality.

I had to let go of past memories, I had to live in the present, I needed to accept my truth, and live in it. In the end it was human company and companionship that meant the most to me. It was the second chance that transformed my life.

Bridesmaids, page boy and flower girl.

Wedding guests.

Hard Truth in Context

Truth is the reality we all live in, but I have discovered that truth is not always easy to accept or digest. Hiding from reality, not disclosing it, and refusing to accept the truth and pretending that all is well is a coping mechanism devised to deal with hard truth. This was my experience for over forty years until the day I opened my Pandora's box and valued what it contained. In actuality I began to realise that truth could not change to suit the feelings and emotions that became a strong part of my existence. I could not unscramble the past, but I could help others as I became willing to show how I grew out of adversity and to learn from what had happened to me. As I look back there was a point when I began to understand that accepting my reality was better than denying it. It was from this vantage point that I began to develop strategies that enabled me to grow out of adversity.

Reflecting on the past I now understand that growing out of adversity is not an overnight thing, but it is a process. It felt natural to want healing to come quickly, but overcoming adversity was a process that occurred over time. As a life coach, I work with others to explain timelines and how important they are in accepting the truth about the past, and how to create a bright future. In reality my past involved many unfavourable experiences, some of which I would rather not have had, but as I think about my life, I know that the adversity I suffered, which is now historic, became a stepping stone for what I am doing at this present time. It increased my capacity to learn, to help others, to live out my purpose and to respond to my highest calling.

In reality, I cannot know what will happen in the future, but I can express hope and visualise what I want to happen. I can do that by setting goals, planning and thinking ahead. I have done it by building on my immense potential and by building on my inner resources. I know that service has been my highest calling and with that calling I have been blessed with skills that have helped others to develop self-confidence. Making a contribution to other people's development and helping them to realise their dreams and ambitions have been of pivotal importance to me.

As I live in my truth, I am able to take one step at a time and it gives me the confidence to keep moving forward with the intention of increasing my capacity to cope with adversity located in the past and the present. Knowing where I am coming from, remembering my roots and not hiding the truth have been a powerful way to overcome adversity. As I accepted truth as it stood, I was able to accept the negatives and with time, grew out of them. At the same time, adversity enabled me to appreciate the many positives of my early life experiences and how in a strange way I was prepared for later traumatic life events. My passion has always been the turning point that drove me forward so that I could associate with key principles that are life sustaining.

The best learning for me is that intense suffering brought a new perspective and a window through which I have been able to look out towards the world and see the many possibilities that could allow me to grow out of adversity. It was the process of learning and growing that helped me to remember that I could be renewed, find new vigour and make sense of my life. I also realised that change would only come as I was challenged to keep moving forward. The key principles I recognised came out of hard truth and then became truth.

Grieving for a loved one requires time to heal. As I was grieving, and going through emotional pain, it felt natural to want to run away, it felt natural to want to hide and even to die. I wanted the pain to end as quickly as it came, but the hard truth was that I needed to be patient and give myself time to heal. I realised that negative feelings, which included blaming, pretending, denial, hiding, holding on to damaging emotions, and refusing to accept the truth, were unhelpful strategies.

The more positive strategy was to possess hope, to seek renewal and the capacity to face life. The hardest truth I had to accept was that if I was going to grow out of my adverse circumstances, I would need to find a level at which I could grow in confidence. I also had to accept that my first love would never return. It was the ability to accept that his loss was out of my hands that enabled me to cope alone.

Finding out about my purpose was closely intertwined with why God allowed me to survive the experiences I encountered. I reasoned that if He allowed me to survive, albeit in a dishevelled state, then there must be a supreme plan that I did not know about. My truth, though hard, allowed me to become a compassionate and caring parent. Of all the things I have done in my lifetime, it is being a mother that is my most enduring achievement. Being a mother was the overarching accomplishment that gave me a sense of gratification, satisfaction and fulfilment.

The only way to discover my purpose was to find something worthwhile on which to focus my mind and my energies. I could only grow through a process of transformed thinking and it resulted in transformation. As Paul the Apostle said,

> And be not conformed to this world: but be ye transformed by the renewing of your mind, that ye may prove what is the good, and acceptable, perfect will of God.
>
> ROMANS 12:2 (HOLY BIBLE)

I returned to the stages of my life where I had failed and took action to improve. The stepping-stone for life purpose was to be on the lookout for where I could make a contribution. I found it was possible to make a contribution in several ways, most notably through parenting, through becoming a professional, through a career in lecturing, mentoring, leadership and life coaching. I found that as I concentrated on others it became the gateway for my personal success.

Thus, the best way to grow out of adversity was to discover my true calling and locate it in an area where I could excel by using the potential that was undiscovered. Less focus on me and more focus on others was the method that created a new future and changed hard truth into truth. The truth was that I was capable of turning around my circumstances by changing the script I had inherited and using it in a way that would enable me to achieve what appeared to be impossible.

Emotional turmoil is an inevitable part of grief and loss. I found that my emotions controlled my thought processes and eventually affected my behaviour, but I am a work in progress, I am not complete, but I find completeness by looking at the life of Jesus and His compassionate approach to others. To be in control of one's emotions and being able to self-regulate is to gain victory over worry, fear and doubt. Worry, fear and doubt had a devastating effect on my psychological state particularly during the early years when I sank into feelings of despair and loneliness.

I found that self-pity and taking on the victim role led to negative emotions. I found it much healthier and more liberating to change my thought processes so that I could find ways to overcome and become resilient during adversity. I realised that my emotions were strongest when I abandoned fear and anxiety and developed trust in God's promises to be with me every step of the way. As a result, I prayed that God would make up for my deficiencies and give me a breakthrough in confidence and determination. I prayed that He would give me wisdom in making wise choices. I prayed that one day he would give me the right partner, not just a partner – and in His time, He did.

My best learning was that I had the power and authority to rise to the many challenges I faced. The realisation that I was more than capable of making decisions and that I could choose which emotions I would accept and those I would reject was the dawning of self-actualisation.

I recognised that I am not an island; I needed others to help and to join with me in being solution-focused. I found that God always provided people upon whom I could depend for unfailing support. I began to see that reciprocal relationships are of key importance. Thus, as I accepted help, I also gave help. I have been blessed with a generous personality so that when I see others in need, I respond with compassion. This way of being connects me with people. My laughter and smile draw others to me, what they see in my eyes tells a story.

The professional training that I completed helped me to become a champion for other people's rights, in particular the rights of children who have suffered abuse, injustice and many kinds of losses. I became a role model and a mentor to others as I befriended them, taught them, and coached them. I gave reassurance and guidance. I emerged out of the struggles I went through at various stages of my life with the capacity to use those experiences in a positive way. In the end it was this lifelong struggle that eventually brought growth. I literally grew out of adversity. Many people have asked me forthrightly, 'how did you do it?'. I simply say I am aspirational; my heart and soul were in the right place and I took initiative at the right time. Nevertheless, I could not have done it on my own, I needed to build positive relationships and this was one of my gifts.

It is impossible to grow out of adversity if there is no light at the end of the tunnel. One of the things I did not want was to be caught up in a cycle of poverty. Thus, it was a pressing concern to look for light while I was in darkness. Growth does not necessarily happen suddenly, but growth materialises out of small efforts that are repeated consistently and with time. A seed that is planted needs light, air, water and the right soil to grow. I could not expect to plant a seed and see growth immediately. Some of the changes I noticed came in spurts and sometimes in an inconsistent pattern. I became more and more inclined to take small steps that would in time be cumulative. Even small changes are good as they bring new possibilities. In reality, I noticed that small changes influenced everything I did thereafter. As I reflect, I am cognisant of the fact that I did not change for the sake of changing, but to be stretched, and to be challenged in order to reach my full potential.

When I showed gratitude, when I spoke to my conscious mind, the changes came not in big waves, but in stillness and quietness. Setting goals was the way I did it. I took time to record my goals, applied time limits, set out a vision and then pushed myself beyond my limits and beyond that of which I felt capable.

One of the goals I made was to become mortgage free. I did not have a partner to contribute to my earnings, but I kept healthy so that I could be self-supporting, and I budgeted, but I did not deny myself. I travelled and have had the privilege of meeting people from all walks of life; I went to the theatre; I went to endless concerts. I saw some of the greatest jazz and classical musicians on stage. I spent time with my family and friends and I did much more. I volunteered within the church community of which I am a member. I know that God has promised to open the windows of heaven and bless all those who give to His cause. I directed my time and my energies wisely; I studied endlessly, seeing learning as lifelong. I focused on what I wanted. I set up my own business and have been successful in maintaining a distinguished career. When I say that I am ready to retire, people protest and say that I still have a lot to give. Yet, I feel contented with the contribution I have made to the lives of countless people whether they were managers, basic-grade social workers, students, course participants, mentees or coaching clients. In this way, I have answered the vital question I posed to myself. What do you ultimately want out of life? It is to feel that I have made the most of the gifts and talents that I have been blessed with, and ultimately to feel that I have made a difference to other people's lives. But my highest and most pre-eminent calling is to know that I reflect the character of Christ in my life. This is my greatest truth and my most diligent purpose.

My personal awareness of my life journey tells me that it was as if I had created a routine that allowed me to move from where I was to where I wanted to be. It took dedication and hard work for small changes to begin showing up, but as I applied the principles of perseverance and determination, I saw what success could look like. I took opportunities as they came and was resolute in following up leads that took me into new and unchartered territories.

At times when I least expected it, my strength became depleted and I often felt discouraged. It is true to say that there were moments when I lost momentum and like a train I was derailed. At these times I applied strategies that allowed the growing process to continue. Seeking spiritual renewal, visualisation and choosing God as a constant companion and friend, increased my inner strength. Renewal came through a spiritual force that was far beyond my human understanding. I prayed and saw amazing answers to prayer. Four of these occasions were the day my son called to say that he had passed his medical examinations; the day he called to say that he had been promoted to Senior Partner in his Practice; the day I received my doctorate; and the day I joined forces with Hubert and was married for a second time. Answer to prayer came when on the one hand I lost my husband and on the other was simultaneously given the gift of my son. I know that these things were not chance happenings, but were part of my destiny. Answer to prayer came when I was unexpectedly given a second chance of a life partner. I have learnt lessons through nature, through exercise, through creative activities, by journaling to access my inner feelings and thoughts. I have found a connection with the God of the universe through diligent Bible study, by listening to uplifting music and through relaxation.

I make it a habit to go on holidays to warmer climates and spend time walking up and down beaches looking for seashells. This is an activity that puts me back in touch with my homeland and my past. It was useful to develop a survival tool kit and in my box of tools were all of the concepts I am explaining.

Throughout my life my truth has been established as a pattern of adversity, but I survived and grew out of adversity and found happiness as I was given many opportunities to use my experience to help others. I did it by accepting what I could not change and living within my truth. I have had a full life and I regret nothing. I fear God and give Him the glory for my modest achievements.

Eight Keys to Wellbeing

There are a number of positive strategies that can be applied to overcome and grow out of adversity and promote wellbeing. These are the keys I frequently used throughout the process of grieving and beyond.

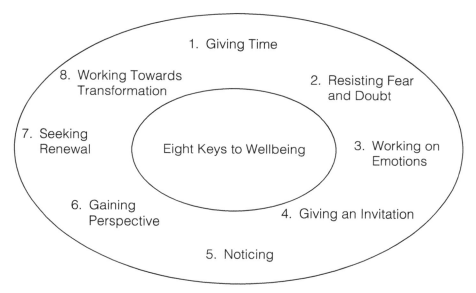

Giving Time

When a person is facing emotional pain and turmoil it is natural to want to speed up the process of healing. He/she knows that others have suffered traumatic life events but never imagined how unbearable it could be. In an effort to ease the pain some people turn to unhealthy methods of coping. Substances, such as alcohol and drugs whether prescribed or illegal, only deaden the pain momentarily and are not the solution. We need to give it time to allow healing to take place. So be patient, and eventually the darkness will fade and the light will come and you will grow out of the pain. I found that time was the best healer.

Resisting Fear And Doubt

Overcoming negative thoughts is essential, because fear and doubt can erode confidence, making it impossible to capitalise on the achievements we have made. The more we engage in negative thoughts, the more the brain engages in negative responses.

> 'As a man thinketh in his heart, so is he.'
>
> PROVERBS 23:7 (HOLY BIBLE)

Fear can easily take over as a response to emotional pain and suffering, but hope and self-belief can come as you change your mindset and bring it under subjection. Look after your mental, physical, spiritual and emotional health. Avoid becoming disconnected from others, but interact socially and engage in exercise. Avoid drugs and alcohol and eat a balanced diet. Each of these actions will lead to optimal health. One of my tools was to remember the importance of gratitude. I found that being grateful encouraged more positive thinking. Doubt and fear can be soul destroying and both can create a cycle of negative thinking.

Working On Your Emotions

Work on your emotions, insecurities and fears by becoming emotionally intelligent through taking care of yourself. A balanced diet and regular exercise releases tension and will help you to rise above harmful emotions that tend to overwhelm. Emotions can easily control how we feel, so decide on which emotions you will allow and which you will reject. If you sink into emotions of helplessness, hopelessness or self-pity, they will cloud your vision and your judgement, and stop you from growing out of adversity. One of the emotions I had to work on was fear. I always felt as though I would have to go through the same experience again, particularly when my son was growing up. I breathed a sigh of relief when he had passed the age of twenty-five since that was the age of his father's death. It was only after that time that I began to cautiously let go of the emotions that were holding me back.

Giving an Invitation

Most people like to receive an invitation; it makes them feel wanted and as if they are making a contribution to another person's happiness. Invite others to join you by soliciting their help and support. Remember that 'no man is an island'. We need others to make us complete. In the universe all things are interconnected, therefore we must rely on interdependent relationships. People give cards and flowers at a funeral, but after time has lapsed, they are genuinely afraid to intrude or to upset the bereaved person by reminding them of the loss. However, if you invite family and friends to join you, they will find it easier to offer the support you need.

Noticing

With the passing of time, notice any changes and improvement in your internal world and celebrate them. Notice growth and reflect on how you coped. Ask what tools you have in your toolkit that will help you to notice change. Insight as well as awareness are useful tools that will prepare you for the next or similar experience. I found that as I noticed how I coped with the tragedy I had experienced I could see how I had grown out of adversity. I noticed that I was a resilient person and it helped me to become more confident and self-efficacious. Insight helped me to know when to rely on God and when to take personal responsibility and action. It is important to take one step at a time, and by all means keep moving. I recently heard a story of a boy who had lost his left arm in a road traffic accident. His mother took him to a judo instructor in the hope that he could be entered for competitions. The judo instructor repeatedly taught the boy only one move. He began to win trophies and eventually he won the championships. The boy noticed that he was only taught one move and asked the judo instructor how it was possible to win the championships when he only knew one move. The instructor replied, 'well, son, your opponent did not know how to grab your left arm, so one move was all you needed.'

Gaining Perspective

Death is like looking through a dark glass. It is one of the hard truths that we do not understand. I found that it was easy to lose perspective. I wanted things to be the way they were. Gaining perspective means seeing the world as it really is and not how we would like it to be. I could not turn back the clock, so I had to think in new and different ways in order to create a new perspective. Gaining perspective also helps with moving forward and not becoming stuck in one position. It is like a diamond that has different angles depending on how it is turned to reflect the light, and a different aspect of the diamond will unfold. Allow the light to enter and be your friend. Gaining perspective means looking for ways to turn around adversity so that it changes from adversity to victory.

Seeking Renewal

After bereavement, seek renewal of the body, mind and spirit by applying a method that fits with your emotions and beliefs. I found that daily devotions, relying on the Bible for guidance, reflection and meditation, to be helpful coping strategies. These methods enabled me to renew my thoughts and to be strengthened inwardly as I looked for positive ways to cope with the grief and to grow out of it. Record your thoughts in a journal and you will be surprised when you look back at what has been achieved and the change that has occurred.

Working Towards Transformation

Before we can heal from any form of loss and grief the mind must undergo a process that leads to transformation. It is the way we think that has a powerful impact on our behaviour. Transformation involves making changes at a time when we least want to accommodate change. Transformation came for me when I did not allow disappointment to

192

cloud my vision or my judgement. I was aware of the distress, the anger, the frustration and the fear I felt and was often overtaken by my emotions. I looked beyond these emotions and I made a conscious choice to change around my circumstances. I believed what Solomon said 'As a man thinketh in his heart so is he.' (Proverbs 23:7). In short, I held onto the belief that it was possible to transform my life. Three of the greatest factors in the process of my transformation were insight, intention and mindset. It seems to me that Michael Jackson's song 'Man in the Mirror' is suggesting that if we want to make a difference in the world, we must make personal changes even if we are a 'willow deeply scared' and a 'washed up dream'. Transformation begins with how we think and what we focus on.

> Finally, brethren, whatsoever things are true, whatsoever things are honest, whatsoever things are just, whatsoever things are pure, whatsoever things are lovely, whatsoever things are of good report; if there be any virtue, and if there be any praise, think on these things.
>
> PHILIPPIANS 4:8 (HOLY BIBLE)

Looking Forward

As I look back at the past, I can also look to the future with assurance that I am not alone. It is the past that has made me into the person I am today. I have been chiselled, hammered, moulded and fashioned into a unique person. The opportunity to become a British citizen, experiencing many setbacks while holding onto my ancestral roots, gives me confidence that others can do what I have done. I look at the lives of those who have made a significant contribution to rebuilding post-war Britain and I am proud to be part of that tradition. As I look in the mirror, I see reflected there hope and many possibilities for the years to come.

I am looking to the future with confidence and the certain knowledge that life is not over until it is over. Life is a continuous journey. It is a long-distance race. Retirement will bring new challenges and new opportunities, one of which is to continue sharing my skills and knowledge. Telling my truth was incredibly hard to bring into the open, but with motivation and letting go of the past, I eventually found a way to accept it.

Throughout the journey of telling my story I was able to go back to my Pandora's box. I discovered that what it held was the power of love. My Pandora's box became an amazing journey and an amazing discovery.

Thanks be to God for his indescribable gift.

2 Corinthians 9:15 The (Holy Bible)

Mama at Joy's graduation.

Lynda and Michael, Birmingham University.

Lynda delivers Breakthrough to Success in leadership seminar.

Lynda after giving a keynote speech.

Lynda on a Caribbean cruise.

Meeting with Dame Cressida Dick at a well-being event.

Michael's Graduation.

Bathsheba, Barbados.

References

Bandua, A. (1997) *Self-Efficacy: The Exercise of Control,* New York: WH Freeman.

Bowlby, J. (1973) *Attachment and Loss. Volume II Separation, Anxiety, Anger.* New York: Basic Books.

Cairns, K. and Fursland, E. (2008) *Transitions and Endings.* London: British Association for Adoption and Fostering

Canfield, J. (2015) *The Success Principles:* Harper New York: Collins

Carter, J. Peace Prize (2002) in Pratt, D. (2007) *1,000 Wisest Things Ever Said: Wisdom of the Nobel Prize Winners.* London: Robinson Press.

Cord, B. (1971) *How the West Indian Child is made Educationally subnormal in the British school system.* London: New Beacon Books.

Covey. S. (1989) *The 7 Habits of Highly Effective People: Powerful Lessons in Personal Change.* New York: Fireside.

Crown Copyright (2003) *Every Child Matters* cm 5860

Cusk, R. (2011) *From Liberty and Equality to the Maternal Grind.* In the Review: The Observer April 3rd.

Dicken F. and Dickens J. (1991) *The Black Manager* New York: Amcom.

Douglass, F. In Cheatham, Bell, J. (1995) *Famous Black Quotations.* New York: Warner Book Company Inc.

Dyer, W. (2006) *Everyday Wisdom for Success.* New York City: Hay House, Inc.

Falhberg, V. (1996) *A Child's Journey Through Placement.* London BAAF.

Gardner, C. (2006) *The Pursuit of HappYness.* New York: Harper Collins.

Gibran, K. *The Prophet* (1980) William. London: Heinemann Limited.

Golding, W. (1954) *Lord of the Flies.* London: Faber and Faber.

Hill, N. and Stone, C. (1987) *Success through a Positive Mental Attitude,* New York: Pocket Books.

Hurston, Z. (1995) *Famous Black Quotations* In Cheatham Bell. J. C. (Ed.) New York: Warner Books.

Ince, L. (1998) *Making it Alone.* London: British Agencies for Adoption and Fostering.

Ince, L. (2001) *Promoting Kinship Care: Preserving Family Networks for Black Children of African Origins.* In Broad, B. (ed.) Kinship Care the Placement Choice for Children and Young People. Dorset: Russel House Publishing.

Ince, L. *Young Black People Leaving Care* (2004). In Lewis, V. Kellet, M. Robinson, C. Fraser, S. and Ding, S. (eds.) London: Sage Publications.

Ince, L. *Kinship Care* (2009) Unpublished Thesis submitted to the University of Birmingham for the Degree of Doctor of Philosophy, Birmingham.

King, Martin Luther Jnr. (1963) *"I have a Dream"* Speech March on Washington.

Kubler-Ross, E. and Kessler, D. (2005) *On Grief and Grieving*. London: Simon & Shuster.

Kouzes J. M. and Posner, B. Z. (2001) *The Five Practices of Exemplary Leadership*. New Jersey: Hobroken.

Littlewood, J. (2014) *Aspects of Grief: Bereavement in Adult Life*. London: Tavistock/Routledge.

Mandela, N. Peace Prize 1993 *In Best 1,000 Wisest Things Ever Said. Wisdom of the Nobel Prize Winners*. Pratt, D. (2007) London: The Robinson Press.

Maxwell, J (2012) *The 15 Invaluable Laws of Growth*. New York: Center Street.

Maxwell, J. (2017) *No Limits: Blow the Lid Off Your Capacity*. New York: Hachette Book Group.

Mbiti, J. (1970) *African Religions and Philosophy*. New York: Garden City, Anchor Books.

North Herts Gazette Series July 26, 1973.

Pearson, A. (1994) *Grieving through Loss*. London: Harper Collins.

Petras, K and R (2014) *It Always Seems Impossible Until It's Done*. New York. Workman Publishing:

Selvon, S. *The Lonely Londoners* (1972) London: Longman Caribbean Limited.

Simone, N. (1969) *Young Gifted and Black*. Lyrics by Weldon Irvine. Sony/ATV Music Publishing LLC, Downtown Music Publishing.

Vanzant, I. (1996) *Faith in the Valley: Lessons for Women on the Journey to Peace*. New York: Simon and Schuster.

Winnicott, D. (1988) *Babies and their Mothers*. London: Free Association Press.

Yeung, R. (2012) *You Can Change Your Life*. London: Macmillan.

INTERNET REFERENCES

Adams, B. https://www.azquotes.com/quote/549495. Retrieved 15th May 2020

Carter, H. https://www.goodreads.com/quotes/11036-there-are-only-two-lasting-bequests-we-can-hope-to retrieved 14 May 2020

Jose Ortega Y Gasset https://quotefancy.com/quote/1202058/Jos-Ortega-y-Gasset-All-we-are-given-are-possibilities-to-make-ourselves-one-thing-or (Retrieved 8 August 2021)

Lao Tzu ChineseProverb https://en.wikipedia.org/wiki/*A journey of a thousand miles begins with a single ste*p. Retrieved 20 June 2020

Lincoln, A. https://www.brainyquote.com/quotes/abraham lincoln 121094 (Retrieved 20th June 2020)

Mitchell, M. T. *What gets in the Way of Gratitude?* In Suttie, J. Can Practising Gratitude Boost Nurses' Resilience https://greatergood.berkeley.edu/article/item/what_stops_gratitudeNov 12, 2013 (Retrieved 12 July 2021)

Onderko, K. *What is Trauma* https://integratedlistening.com/what-is-trauma/Retrieved

23rd July 2021.

Roosevelt, F. D. https://quotefancy.com/quote/806496/Franklin-D-Roosevelt-*Go-for-the-moon-If-you-don-t-get-it-you-ll-still-be-heading-for-a* (Retrieved 4 May 2020).

Roosevelt, E. *You Learn by Living*: Eleven Keys for a more fulfilling life https://www.goodreads.com/quotes/3823-you-gain-strength-courage-and-confidence-by-every-experience-in (retrieved 26 January 2020)

Thoreau, H. D. https://www.goodreads.com/quotes/210840-*i-know-of-no-more-encouraging-fact-than-the-unquestionable* (Retrieved 27th January 2020).

Phipps, W. https://www.azquotes.com/author/46675-Wintley Phipps retrieved 26 January 2019

Bible References

KINGS JAMES VERSION

Proverbs 25:11

Ecclesiastes 3:1

1 Timothy 6:7

Ecclesiastes 1:9

Revelation 21:4

Proverbs 4: 6-7

Daniel Chapter 3:17-18

Zechariah 4:6

Proverbs 13:20

Proverbs 18:24

Romans 11:33

Deuteronomy 33:27

Ruth 1: 1-5

Psalms 23:1-4

Luke 11:9-10

James 2:17

Romans 5 1-5

Proverbs 3: 5-6

11 Corinthians 12:9

Mark 6:31

1 Peter 5: 6-7

11 Timothy 2:15

Job 23:10

1 Corinthians 15:58

Isaiah 55: 8-9

1 John 4:18

Romans 12:2

Proverbs 23:7

Philippians 4:18

11 Corinthians 9:15